Kevin,

Sul best wishes,

Eric, or Little by Little

Eric Hughes

authorHOUSE®

AuthorHouse™ UK Ltd.
500 Avebury Boulevard
Central Milton Keynes, MK9 2BE
www.authorhouse.co.uk
Phone: 08001974150

First published by AuthorHouse 5/25/2010

ISBN: 978-1-4520-0937-7 (sc)

This book is printed on acid-free paper.

This book is dedicated to my wife, Doris Helena, for her love, support and understanding in putting up with me over the years.

FOREWORD

In *Eric, or Little by Little,* I have concentrated on portraying my personal and business escapades from 1929 through to 2008, sprinkled with sporting memories. Unusually, I have described my *Life in Athletics* separately, as it would have been too complicated to intertwine certain recorded facts in one book without distracting from the flow of events.

Eric Hughes

1

My life began in 1929 in a small back street in Higher Broughton, Salford, in a house without a bathroom and an outside WC in the backyard. We could not afford toilet paper, so old newspapers were cut into squares and secured by a nail behind the door. On freezing winter nights, when it was too cold to venture out, a bucket was employed at the rear door of the scullery and emptied early the following morning. Saturday night was bath night, taking place in a large zinc tub in front of an open coal fire that heated pans of water. There was always food on the table, and our treat was stewed rabbit, skinned and supplied by a local shopkeeper.

The house was in the shadow of a burned-out rubber factory close to wasteland known locally as 'The Hills,' and strangely enough an elderberry tree somehow grew through the paving stones of the backyard. Once a year, gypsies would call and trade donkey stones for the blossoms from the tree, which they would covert into some form of health potion. In those days, donkey stones, a form of sandstone, mostly in cream, were used by proud housewives to scour their front door steps and sometimes window sills as a form of decoration in competition with their neighbours.

My grandmother Donovan lived close by, and following the early passing of her husband, a well- known bookie, she shared her house with the Morrison family. Pop Morrison was a widower and a former Sergeant Major in the Army. He had a waxed moustache, a gravelly voice, and literally swore like a trooper. Granny 'Donny' was an enormous woman, over twenty stone, who downed pints of beer with her drinking partner,

Pop, but had a heart of gold. She was also extremely thrifty and once sent me on an errand over a mile away to a greengrocer with a reputation for good value. Upon my return, with a bag of potatoes, carrots, and onions, she found that she had been overcharged a penny, and I had to cover the distance again with a note of complaint. When I got back with the penny, she gave me tuppence for going.

In contrast, my other granny, Granny Hughes, was small and thin, also being widowed prematurely. She lived with her spinster sister, Ellen, bringing up my father in Brook's Bar, South Manchester, in a very sombre environment.

My mother, Marion, met my father, Ted, when she nearly poked his eye out with an umbrella outside a dance hall. They were married for almost fifty years, always sacrificing themselves for their children.

When the Jewish immigrants arrived in this country from Russia in the early 1920s, they settled in the Higher Broughton area, bringing with them their crafts and skills, particularly in sewing and garment making. So I was brought up in a Jewish community with my sister, Marjorie, who had been born on exactly the same day in February, three years earlier. At a young age, I learned the art of bargaining from my friend Marty Segal, the son of a watchmaker, and became expert in trading cigarette cards and marbles.

My father had lost his job in the recession during the early 1930s and had become a street lamp lighter. To make ends meet, my mother went to work for a garment manufacturer, rising to the position of supervisor. The children were looked after by Granny Donny and Pop, who picked us up from school in an old lorry.

I was then a miserably thin specimen with steel glasses and a patch over one eye, and I was an obvious target for the bullies at the primary school I attended in Cheetham Hill. Much to the disappointment of my father, who had played amateur soccer, I had no interest in sports whatsoever.

My sister Jean was born in 1936, and in 1938, when I was nine years old, my Uncle Harry accepted a job in Gibraltar and offered to rent the Hughes family his house in Moss Side. This meant us moving from North Manchester to the south side, but to a home with hot water, a bathroom, and indoor toilet. It was a dream come true. The house was terraced and situated just off Princess Road, close to Alexandra Park, and I went to Princess Road Primary School. My weekly pleasure was going to bed to read second hand comics in a room of my own, accompanied by six rounds of toast and dripping.

When war broke out in 1939, children were hurriedly evacuated, and I landed up in Cheadle Hulme. Today this is only ten minutes by car, but in those days it appeared a million miles away, and ironically the first bomb in the northwest was dropped close by. On the other hand, Doris, my wife to be, at the age of seven years had been dispatched to Cheddleton in Staffordshire, forty miles away, with her two sisters. There she saw a cow for the first time, and for four-and-a-half years grew up in hard, but healthy village surroundings.

I was occasionally allowed home, and during the Christmas break of 1939, I can vividly remember walking all the way to Salford with my mother through a blitzed Manchester city centre to find out if my grandmother was still alive. The experience was unforgettable, with buildings burning around us, debris everywhere, and anxious faces looking up to the skies, wondering when the next air raid would occur.

Life in the country was certainly different, and after a disastrous first billet, where I had to suffer a cold water bath every night, I was lucky enough to share a home with a lovely old couple who treated me very well. By making a fresh start and having to fend for myself, my confidence grew, but apart from being able to run naturally, I still had no interest in sport. There was great rivalry between the evacuees and local children, and based on the legend of Robin Hood (me as Robin) I led the townies to glory in an almighty battle on the fields of Cheadle Hulme. Some sixty years later, Doris and I were leaving an antiques fair in Cheshire when I heard a voice behind me singing, "Robin Hood, Robin Hood and his band of men..." and when I looked around there stood Stan Seddon, one of the 'Merry Men' with whom I was evacuated, recalling the 'epic' so long ago.

We evacuees attended a local school, and in the spring we were required to sit for a secondary school examination. Surprisingly, I passed for a central school, a division between elementary and grammar school education, meaning I had to return home in 1940 to attend St Margaret's in Whalley Range.

The war was still raging, and the family, together with the cat, spent most nights huddled in a brick air-raid shelter located in the backyard, alerted by the wail of sirens and the noise of overhead German aircraft. Incendiary bombs and shrapnel constantly rained down, and on one occasion, the nearby corner shop suffered a direct hit. My father was constantly on ARP duty (Air Raid Precaution), and we always breathed a sigh of relief when he came home in one piece.

September arrived and I enrolled at St Margaret's in an old school building close to the church, about a mile from Russell Street where I lived. Due to war service, the age of teachers ranged from a French teacher in her late teens to a science teacher in his mid-sixties, whose favourite expression to silence pupils was to brandish a ruler saying, "Be quiet or I will strike your hand with timber." My favourite subject was art, and I got by in the other subjects, but when the day came for sport, I froze.

Whenever the afternoon came along to depart for the nearby playing fields, I always had an excuse ready not to participate. I got away with this until the last day of the football season, at the end of the spring term, when the sports teacher got hold of me and made it clear that whatever the reason I had to offer, I was going to take part in a game.

There I stood on a soccer field for the first time, frightened out of my wits and with no idea of the rules, except that the ball had to go between two posts to score. When the opportunity came my way I did just that, but to my horror I had put the ball through my own net. It was bad enough dodging over the months, but this incident made me the laughing stock of the school, and to say I was ridiculed was a gross understatement.

I made my way home feeling suicidal, and because no one was in, I sat on the top of the front step feeling thoroughly miserable and sobbing my heart out. Then came a moment that was to change my entire life, when a voice said, "What's the matter son?" There stood a man in a RAF uniform who had called to see a friend next door. He sat on the step next to me whilst I poured my heart out, and listening patiently he said, "You can do one of two things, either you give up or you learn to play football and prove yourself." "How could I possibly do that?" I replied and he said that if I was to dedicate myself and work very hard, he would help me. He returned the following day with an exercise book filled with ideas on how I could progress. He pointed out that I did not have the physique to be a defender and that I should concentrate on ball playing and derived the exercises accordingly.

One idea was to find a wall (I found one in a local school playground) and hit a tennis ball against it without touching the ground. Another was to place objects (I used to practise on the park rec with bricks) and swerve in and out with either foot. Another was to run with a tennis ball, passing this from foot to foot, plus many other exercises. Summer school holidays were just beginning and I devoted every hour of every day practising. At first, it was very difficult, but gradually my skill developed, and after months of perseverance, I could hit a tennis ball against the wall over fifty times and could swerve between the bricks at speed. Each morning I dribbled a tennis ball on my paper round, moving from house to house, up and down drives, and began to feel the thrill of ball control.

Taking the story a step forward, when for the first time I watched Manchester City play at Maine Road, I was amazed to see the man in the RAF uniform leading City out. He was none other than the great Peter Doherty, a famous international and one of the finest players of all time to wear City's colours. Peter was my father's idol and I will never forget what he did for me.

I could not wait for school to begin, and when the day for sports arrived, I made the usual half-hearted excuses. The same teacher demanded I should play and put me in a third-ranked match. This was what I had been waiting for, and to the amazement of all I scored six goals (against weak opposition). The following year, I captained the school team.

The headmaster of St Margaret's did not approve and told me that I was not one of his favourites, but maybe 'little by little' I might get there.

My whole life had changed, my confidence soared, and I believed I could do anything. I even conquered my fear of the dark by climbing over the park gates at night.

2

I became obsessed with football and played every available moment I could. In the school breaks matches were organised in Alexandra Park using a patched up old case ball with as many as fifteen to twenty on each side. These games sometimes lasted for three hours nonstop, then we changed the teams and started again. This improved my stamina and ball control, and I became recognised locally as a decent player. Among the other youngsters who took part in these matches were Dennis Violet (he succeeded me as school captain), Dougie Holden, and Billy Myerscough, all of whom made their mark in the professional game.

Time rolled by, and I needed to start thinking about my future career; my ambition was to work in the world of art, which appeared to be inherent throughout my family. My father painted scenes in water colours; my sister Marjorie later exhibited her work, and Stephen, my son, achieved an 'A' level in art. My speciality was cartoons, and after an interview with the principal of the College of Art in Manchester, I was told that my work was good, but not good enough. The prospects in this field were extremely limited due to the shortage of paper because of the war, and there was very little commercial opportunity.

This was disappointing, and I felt that the next best opening would be to train as a draughtsman, where I could at least draw, and I was offered an apprenticeship in an engineering company in Parrswood with a wage of 14s 8d (old money) each fortnight. To save the pennies I would walk the four miles back and forth each day and cut the lawns of local houses in my lunchtime. Obviously, being a fourteen-year-old, I was a general dogsbody and gradually became disillusioned with both the prospects and nature of the trade. A few months passed, and I realised there was no real connection with creative art, and putting myself in the place of the chairman (the ultimate goal), I decided to call it a day.

With no idea just what to do, I applied in writing for ten positions advertised in the Manchester Evening News which included timber, coal, insurance, shipping, and textiles and was granted nine interviews. My minimum wage demand was the princely sum of twenty shillings (£1.00) per week and this appeared to be an acceptable option.

The last of my interviews was in a first floor office in Mosley Street, the company concerned being involved in the export of textiles. Being shown into the manager's office, I was confronted by a small, plump, red-faced man eating tripe with a glass of beer at his elbow. For a while he ignored me then, with his mouth full of tripe, he started to ask me questions. My blood boiled at such rudeness, and I told him that even a boy of my age deserved some respect; I stated that I would not be interested in working with such a bad-mannered person and duly left the building. When I got home, I was still furious at the treatment I had received and vowed that even if I was offered a fortune, it would be the last job I would consider.

During the next few days, I received five offers at £1.00 per week. The best offer came from the textile company, at £1.50, with a letter from the manager who had interviewed me initially, Jack Crossland, stating that he admired my spirit. I was about to tear the letter up when my mother asked me to give him a chance, as he would not have offered me more if he did not think something of me. To please her I agreed 'to give it a go' on the condition that I would leave if I was unhappy after a trial period.

The following Monday morning, with some trepidation, I reported for my first day at the Allied National Corporation; the office in Mosley Street was a Manchester branch set up in the heart of the textile trade with the intention of locating supplies. As the office boy, I was expected to undertake any menial job, including filing, making tea, and running errands (which included going for tripe at the UCP in Piccadilly each Friday). After getting to know my new surroundings, I was shown to a small anteroom filled from floor to ceiling with masses of papers, with the instruction, "Sort them and file them." The papers mostly consisted of letters and copy indents accumulated from all over the world, in no particular order. This constituted quite a challenge, and gradually I developed a system of filing by country or supplier, alphabetically for each section, taking in names and whereabouts in the process. I became so engrossed with the task that three months had gone by and I was learning something about the business and found the world of textiles to be fascinating.

The war was over and there was a general shortage of goods everywhere, in particular countries of what was at the time the British Empire such as Australia, New Zealand, South Africa, and the West Indies. The purpose of Allied National was to discover any form of textiles in this country, add a profit, and cable out the relevant details to appointed overseas agents, including the total value of the offer. Nine times out of ten, there would be an acceptance, together with notification that a letter of credit would be issued in advance to cover the requisition. All manner of goods were involved, but the principle demand was for cloth, and this was a speciality of Jack Crossland, who knew the weaving trade inside out. Most of the transactions were carried out in the Circus Tavern in Portland Street where Jack met daily with his cronies, and he would return to the office with a few pints down him to arrange cable offers.

Even at a young age I eventually became expert in compiling these cables and monitoring the transactions, continually adding to my knowledge. Exotic locations in such places as South Africa and the West Indies stuck in my mind, and little did I realise that some time in the future I would be visiting these countries in a different capacity.

I enrolled at the Manchester College of Technology and spent two evenings each week studying spinning, weaving, and textile design, supplementing technical knowledge to practical experience.

Football occupied most of my social life and a new soccer club was formed at the Wilbraham Road Community Centre under the name of Wilbraham FC, enlisting in a local open-age league. Although only fifteen, I was invited to join the team, which included my future brother in law, Bill Hunt, and a squad of fully grown men. I was still of slender build, and after weeks of being kicked and mauled every match, I was advised to play in a league more suited to my age level. One of the top young teams at the time was the Manchester YMCA, who were in the Lads Federation League, and included Dougie Holden and his brothers and a number of other friends from my park days. After signing on, I found this much more enjoyable and I settled down at inside forward, most of the fixtures being in North Manchester.

As Old Trafford had suffered war damage, Manchester United shared Maine Road with City, and there were attendances of over 60,000 at each match. Most of the crowds stood on the terraces, and there was virtually no trouble with spectators, although on several occasions more than 80,000 people were present. Sometimes youngsters were passed overhead from hand to hand to the safety of the front of the playing area. It was a regular practice to wait outside the ground until the gates were opened at three-quarter time for us to nip in and see the rest of the game free.

City's good neighbour gesture eventually worked against them, as United, under the early management of Matt Busby, developed into the better team and supporters followed them back to Old Trafford when it reopened.

For exercise and to save money, I walked to and from work each day and was sent on minor missions to companies around Manchester collecting samples. I gradually made contacts using my early age Jewish bargaining powers to my advantage. Having enjoyed a certain amount of success, Jack Crossland decided to send me further afield, such as catching an early morning bus to the Colne and Nelson areas and tramping miles from mill to mill seeking supplies. This was extended to my very first overnight business trip to Nottingham, where I stayed at a hotel for the first time, eating dinner in the dining room, and working out which knife and fork to use. I covered a wide area by bus or on foot in the underwear district of Britain and returned home with offers of hosiery, vests, and so forth; my biggest acquisition was a huge quantity of French knickers with slack elastic. Details were in turn relayed overseas and resulted in substantial orders being placed. As time progressed, I undertook more and more responsibility, which left

Jack Crossland more drinking time; by the time I was eighteen, I was virtually doing his job.

I have been fortunate enough to escape with my life on a number of occasions, but foremost in my mind was at a soccer FA Cup sixth round match between Bolton and Stoke at Burnden Park, Bolton in 1946. In those days, standing was permissible, and iron barriers were situated on the steps of the terraces to divide and ease crowd pressure. The match was sold out, and disappointed spectators began clambering over fencing at the railway end, at the back of the kop, where I stood about a third of the way from the pitch. More and more people foolishly followed suit, and this resulted in hundreds of spectators being crushed. I, for one, finished up doubled over a completely bent barrier and did not realise until later that thirty-three people had been killed just in front of me. Also, over five hundred people were injured, and to this day the tragedy is still known as the 'Bolton Disaster'. I had no idea of the seriousness of the situation until I was told by the famous City goalkeeper, Frank Swift, on the train going home. My parents had heard the news earlier over the radio, had been out of their minds with worry, and needless to say were relieved to see me.

Meanwhile I was earning a decent reputation in soccer with several professional scouts showing interest, and I was invited for a trial at Stockport County.

3

Conscription into the Forces in those days was compulsory and although Allied National applied for my exemption, after a while this was rejected. In 1947, I was drafted into the RAF, reporting for duty at Padgate, near Warrington.

There did not appear to be any practical area to further my textile career, but I quickly learned that if you were good at either sport or music, life could be bearable. As I could not even play a mouth organ, sport, and in particular soccer, appeared to be the best option, and after a few days of joining up, I found myself in the Station team. I soon made friends with Tony Hapgood, the son of the famous Eddie Hapgood, the former England captain of Arsenal fame, and lads from various parts of the country.

I did not realise at the time, but I had developed a big head, and being a member of Her Majesty's forces certainly brought me down to earth with a bang. It toughened my character and taught me much about human nature, which, in itself, was an invaluable lesson.

About thirty of us shared a Nissen hut on my first night at Padgate, and after lights out, a very drunk Scotsman wandered from bed to bed complaining that he could not sleep. This went on for ages, begging someone to hit him and put him out of his misery. No one reacted, and feeling tired and fed up, I duly obliged and at last peace reigned. However, in the early hours of the morning I was suddenly awakened by a furious bleary eyed Scot holding a bayonet at my throat, shouting, "Are you the f— Sassenach who hit me?"

Although I was awarded various privileges through sport, the pay was not very good, and I received a small income by charging for photographing recruits in their new uniforms for them to send home.

Square bashing (marching and drills) were certainly not my scene, having two left feet, but somehow I completed the course and passed out as a fully fledged airman.

I needed to decide on which branch of the RAF I should concentrate, which was mainly a question of where I could undertake minimum duties yet still specialise in sport. Three choices were open to me, the Special Police, Medical, or Dental, and I did not fancy the cropped hair and white gaiters that were part of a SP role. As most of the Medical staff appeared to be gay, I enrolled on a dental hygienist course at RAF Halton, and once qualified, this gave me the opportunity to be excused from duty whenever the occasion arose.

Bridgenorth in Shropshire was my first major posting, and to add to my playing and training for the Station and the Command, I was approached to join Walsall, which was managed by Harry Hibbs, another soccer legend. On Saturday nights, I mixed with the Wolverhampton Wanderers team at the weekly town hall dance and got to know Billy Wright, Ron Flowers, and other members of the Club.

My general physical fitness had never been better and I was invited by the Station to run in the Bridgenorth-Wolverhampton marathon. I have always liked and been interested in athletics, and I had run a 4 minute 10 second mile, this being largely due to a natural slow pulse rate that gave me extra stamina. With basically little training, I actually won the race in 2 hours 33 minutes and upon crossing the finishing line, I was congratulated by the medical officer, who added that I must have spent a considerable amount of time in preparation. When I told him this was not the case, he immediately ordered me to hospital, where I spent a number of painful days recovering, my ribs contracting almost to breaking point. This was my one and only marathon.

Life was enjoyable at Bridgenorth, and true to belief, I did get a lot of time off for training, playing, and travelling constantly to other RAF units when we would always be entertained with great food after each match.

Midweek matches were arranged with various soccer clubs in the Midlands, one particular fixture being with the Stafford Rangers. Before each game I always weighed up the opposition and was pleased to see a thin, gangly wing half with bandy legs had the job of marking me. I could not have been more wrong. Not only did he put me in his pocket, but contributed to all six Stafford goals. Years later I was to see him in Manchester City colours being regarded as one of the best uncapped player ever, and Ken Barnes went on to become a vital part of the Revie plan, earning him a 1956 Cup Winners medal. I still see Ken regularly at the City Stadium and often remind him of the incident.

I became reasonably proficient in my official capacity, and as an earner, I followed lectures given on dental hygiene with the unofficial sale of toothbrushes after scaring those present half to death that their teeth would drop out if they did not brush regularly.

Sadly my life in Shropshire came to an abrupt end. I was always suspicious that the medical hospital sergeant was homosexual, and by chance I came across him at the back of his billet 'in action' with another. He spotted me, and in order to shut me up he arranged for an immediate posting to RAF Horsham St Faith outside Norwich, the other side of the country.

Upon arrival I was summoned by the sports officer, who was already in possession of my CV, and I was immediately selected for the Station soccer team. Contrary to Bridgenorth, Horsham St Faith was a small former fighter station situated on an airfield a short distance outside the city. It offered a much more relaxed atmosphere, and eventually I moved into an unused hospital room close to the surgery, and was served early morning cups of tea by WAAF nurses. I could hop out of a ground floor window on to a disused runway, ideal for training, with a sports ground also close by.

For a while I trained at Norwich City at Carrow Road, but on the advice of several of my RAF colleagues, I signed for Great Yarmouth FC in the Southern league. East Anglia was starved of soccer and the following of nonleague was amazing. I made my debut in March 1949 against Gorleston (managed by Sailor Brown, the former Charlton Athletic star), a local derby match, attended by no fewer than 10,000 spectators with a great atmosphere. If you played well, you became a hero with headlines in the Saturday Pink, and weekend passes and expenses were thrown into the package.

Great Yarmouth reached the Southern Cup Final and was drawn against Arsenal at Carrow Road, Norwich, on a Wednesday evening. There followed one of the blackest days in my soccer career. One of my RAF responsibilities was to accompany the dental officer around the smaller stations in the fens, and I applied for exemption on the day of the final so that I could adequately prepare myself. The officer concerned hated sport and not only refused my request, but deliberately delayed my return to the Norwich region. He eventually dropped me about two miles away at 7.00 p.m., the kick off being at 7.30 p.m., and I had to run the distance all the way, arriving in the dressing room exhausted and obviously very upset. The team were stripped for action, and I was devastated to learn that the first reserve had injured himself in the warm-up, and I had no alternative but to play in a state of fatigue. My performance was dreadful, made worse by a nightmare of missing an easy open goal, which would have equalised Arsenal's only score which won the Cup. I offered my loser's medal to the injured reserve, and to this day I feel bad that I let a great club and a wonderful bunch of lads down.

In the summer of 1949, I was finally routed to RAF Warton, near Blackpool, to be demobbed (demobilised) and was issued with my civvy (civilian) suit in blue serge.

4

Shortly after settling down at home a number of soccer scouts were knocking at the door. Although my father and I were 'blue' through and through, we had not heard good news about the internal running of Manchester City, so I accepted an invitation to train with Burnley. They had a reputation for being one of the best clubs in the country for the development of young players, and I made my way to Turf Moor twice a week on a North Western single-decker bus from Mosley Street. Everything I had heard about Burnley was true, and I thoroughly enjoyed the coaching and encouragement I received, which led to me being chosen for the public trial prior to the first league fixture. In the days of overpaid millionaire footballers, it is refreshing to remember that my selection card stated, 'please bring your own towel and shin pads'. In those days there were no friendly previews, and the first team attack faced the first team defence, that is, the Blues vs the Clarets. A large crowd assembled and I was having a good game until I collided with Strong, the goalkeeper, on the near post and was carried off. This put an end to my early ambitions, and for some time I travelled for treatment to Burnley by bus across the moors twice a week, returning home late at night. After a while this became very tiring, particularly in bad weather, added to the fact that I needed constant attention to my injury. As I had not officially registered with Burnley, I was still a free agent and a scout from City continually pestered me to join. My home in Moss Side was only a stone's throw from Maine Road. In a weak moment I agreed and signed for manager Sam Cowan, the former cup winning captain and a hero of my father's.

I wasted little time getting back to work; Allied National was now known as Barrow Platt and had moved to larger premises in Princess Street. In my absence, the staff had multiplied, and it was a question of my starting all over. A small office with no windows was allocated to me, and I quickly discovered a distinct change in the character of the business. Exports at any price were quickly coming to an end as most overseas countries were now re-establishing their own industries. Also a good deal of speculation had taken place in anticipation of orders that never came and the warehouse stock was considerable. With reduced export opportunities and no home market connections, the company was suddenly in difficulties.

There was anger and resentment by UK buyers against companies such as Barrow Platt for long ignoring this country in favour of export profit making, but this was the only option open to us, and I volunteered to attempt selling the stock in the home market. The company agreed to this, and I spent two days in Central Library listing potential customers from Plymouth to Aberdeen who were, in those days, mostly wholesalers. Armed with a case of samples, I set about my journeys to all areas of Great Britain, travelling by third class rail, bus, and foot. The reception I received was hostile to say the least, but gradually I began to make headway, keeping careful records and details of my calls.

Upon reaching Scotland I cultivated a very useful technique. Calling at Hunter Barr, a famous Glasgow wholesale company, I was given a horrendous blast by the buyer concerned and left his office feeling exhausted and demoralised. I had had enough and sat on the steps outside the building in Queen Street close to tears when a voice asked me why I was so upset. It was the buyer who had just slated me and after I had stuttered an explanation of a young man desperate for business he asked me to return after lunch. I hung around and eventually came away with an order and from then onwards I adopted the Pagliacci method whenever the occasion arose. Pagliacci was famous as a grief-stricken clown in Ruggero Leoncavallo's opera who had to go on stage despite being heartbroken, always winning the sympathy of the audience.

At last all the stock was gone, with the exception of one thousand ATS knickerbockers, which I sold to the Arabs for keeping sand off their knees.

During my home market pilgrimage, it was apparent that there was a major demand for curtaining fabrics, so I set about finding appropriate supplies. Once sourced, I added a profit. Then, using the contacts I had made on my travels, approached the relevant buyers and gradually built a reasonable turnover.

After leaving the RAF I was reunited with my friends, John Andrews, Colin Fletcher, and Norman Blake, in the days of the big bands that played at various venues in the Manchester area. These included the High Street Baths, where a dance floor was built over the swimming area, Belle Vue, The Ritz, and Plaza in the city centre and, above all, the Levenshulme Palais. I had taken limited ballroom lessons at Cowans Academy in Moss Side and was familiar with most of the basic steps, because at the time, dancing was the favourite pastime for meeting people. Except for Sundays, the Palais was open every night to the music of Bill Edge and his band, and it was there that I first saw Doris, my wife to be. I noticed this beautiful, slim girl with long dark hair standing near a doorway, and although I did not dance with her on the night, the picture of her remained with me. Shortly afterwards, we met briefly at a social club on Hall Lane, Fallowfield, in September 1949. This was run by the Co-op, and on Sundays in particular, the facilities were amazing, but very affordable. I came across Doris again, seated by a roaring coal fire, knitting. I have only lit up a cigarette once in my life, and it was on that night, for fun. I half-smoked a long seven-inch fag, and this was the first sight Doris had of me. She must have thought 'what a wally'. The next time was when we first danced together at the Palais, and I learned that I had asked her sister Marie out, but neither of us showed up. This happened to be a good thing, as there was a pledge between the sisters not to go on dates with the same boy. After walking Doris home the next night, we found we had a lot in common, including both having a black cat called Tiggy, yet we were totally different in personality.

On our first date, we went to the town pictures to see 'Jake', a horror feature at the Gaiety on Peter Street, long since demolished. It was also a horror for us when, being seated in a very steep balcony, I dropped a bag of Maltesers at a very tense moment in the film and the hushed silence was broken by the noise of Maltesers tip-topping from stair level to stair level. It was embarrassing at the time, but it created a memory we still recall today. We both became regular Palais goers and met there sometimes three or four times a week, Doris being a natural dancer who liked to sweep around the large ballroom floor.

Our backgrounds were very similar, and we both knew hardship. Doris lived in a council house in Longsight, and I lived in a terraced house in Moss Side; both of our parents had little money. My father worked night shifts in a power sub station at that time, and Doris's father was a printer in the newspaper industry. He was a disciple of Churchill and lived in fear of the atomic bomb, his favourite expression after visiting the pub was 'one flash, all ash'.

Our relationship grew, but money was always short, and a typical evening was to play draughts at Happy's (a snack bar in Rusholme), making a cup of coffee last for hours thanks to the sympathetic café owner. We both walked to and from work to save the pennies, and I always hiked the three miles home from Longsight, passing Maine Road on my way. Sometimes, well after midnight, I would slink past the ground with my collar pulled up high feeling self conscious, being very much aware of the club's early-to-bed rule. This was in distinct contrast to me turning in each night at 9.30 p.m. in preparation for an early morning run in the local park accompanied by Rover, the best football dog in the land. Jimmy McClelland, the City coach, constantly lectured the young players on a possible drop in form, his three principle reasons for this being, smoking, drinking, or women. Once, after having a poor match, he asked me, "Which of the three is it, Hughes?"

My injury had cleared and I worked with the semi-professionals on Tuesdays and Thursdays. Sam Cowan had been replaced as manager by Jock Thompson. By today's standards, training was pathetic, consisting of a few laps of the pitch and a game of indoor five side soccer in a white washed corridor under the stand. A huge red headed giant of a man, Dave Ewing, had just joined the club from Scotland and although Dave was a gentle, quiet person in everyday life, he was a killer once he got involved with a football. His favourite trick was to let you pass him, then jam your head against the railings that separated the corridor. I woke up half unconscious in the dressing rooms on more than one occasion.

Another newcomer was a blond, impressive, former German paratrooper named Bert Trautmann, who of course became a City goal keeping legend. My memory of Bert was different from so many others when he played in the 1956 Wembley Cup Final with a broken neck. After training one night, I was furiously rubbing dubbin into a new pair of boots to soften the leather when Bert came up with a different recipe. "If you p-- [urinate] on the boots," he said, "that will do the trick," adding that he had done this himself in the backyard of his adopted home in St Helens, much to the disgust of his future in-laws who almost threw him out. It worked and this became the practice whenever I bought new boots.

My Father was proud of me playing in City colours and had always reminisced about the blues' pre-war cup victory; I felt very humble that two of his heroes, Len Barnett and Freddie Tilson, who had played in the final, had to clean the baths and tidy up after us.

5

During my mission to locate curtaining fabrics, I came across a particularly attractive floral design. After obtaining samples, I sold a considerable amount of cloth to my contacts in all parts of Great Britain.

In turn, the supplier was able to place large print orders, beyond his wildest dreams, delivering the goods to the Barrow Platt warehouse for distribution to my wholesale customers. The supplier concerned was H Black (Textiles) Ltd, who operated as a job merchant from a cellar in an unlikely address at St James Street, by the side of the Odeon cinema. Harry Black, the proprietor, was larger than life and the perfect loveable rogue; his main business was to serve market traders who paid their bills in bank notes, generally wrapped up in old newspapers. The design that linked us came his way because of his association with a well-known printer who was delighted with the volume of orders that had suddenly transpired. It became necessary for me to call regularly at St James Street to monitor transactions, and in time, the friendship between Harry and myself grew.

The management and coaching strategy at Manchester City left a lot to be desired; although I loved the club, I was not very happy. Ball control, which was the best feature of my play, was not encouraged, and the accent was on the physical side of the game. I still remained an amateur, being a brown envelope footballer receiving a worthwhile amount if I played well and just my bus fare if I did not.

In August 1950, things began looking up when Leslie McDowell arrived as the new manager. He gathered everyone at the training ground on Wilbraham Road for a new beginning, with concentration on pure football. The Revie plan was eventually adopted, with Don as the deep lying centre forward working in harmony with the brilliant Ken Barnes at wing half, the object being to feed strikers Jack Dyson and Joe Hayes, supported by hard-working wingers. Johnnie Williamson understudied the Don and I was asked to fill the role at a lesser level, and for a while I enjoyed myself again. Most of the A team games were staged behind the Butchers' Arms venue in Droylesden. The kit man at the time was little Albert Alexander, who later became one of the best loved chairmen in the Mercer-Allison era. Looking back, it was quite a privilege to have him handing out the kit and collecting the dirty washing, not forgetting lighting and heating a large boiler for the after match bath. Nothing was too much trouble for Albert in those early days or in his highly prestigious office during one of the most successful periods in the Club's history.

Learning of my general unrest, yet another scout contacted me and enquired if I would like to turn out for Notts County, and if so, he could arrange for me to play in mid week matches. Jack Crossland initially agreed for me to take days off during January–March 1951 when I travelled to Meadow Lane and played in the company of the famous, but aging legends Tommy Lawton and Len Luty. Due to some members of staff at Barrow Platt objecting, my Wednesday excursions were abruptly ended, but another opportunity came my way out of the blue.

Louis Rocca, the well known chief scout of United, appeared at the front door of Russell Street one night and asked if I would like a trial at Old Trafford. Because of the fierce traditional rivalry between the two clubs, I found this unbelievable and, in a way, laughable. But I knew Dennis Violet and a number of the United lads, and they persuaded me to give it a try. Tongue in cheek, I duly reported at Old Trafford on a Wednesday afternoon to take part in a practice match and was placed in the first team attack alongside former international stars such as Jimmy Delaney, Stan Pearson, and Charlie Mitten. Anyone who has played football knows that at certain times in their career they have days when everything goes right. This was one of those days for me when, in spite of Billy (Killer) McGlen being elected to mark me and rough me up, I had one of the best games of my life. I was switched to the reserve attack against the first team defence in the second half and still held my own.

After the match, Jimmy Murphy, the United assistant team manager, sought me out and asked if I could attend training the following Tuesday evening. This was somewhat embarrassing as, even if I had been offered the chance, I would never have gone to United and had only accepted their first approach in devilment. Encouraged by Dennis and other pals on the Red side of town, I took matters a stage further. When I turned up on the Tuesday, Jimmy Murphy took me out on the pitch and aimed balls at me from all angles, watching my reactions and noting my ball control. When finished, he said, "Not bad. You had better have a word with the boss (Matt Busby), and by the way, how old are you?" When I replied that I was in my early twenties he retorted, "Forget it," and walked away, leaving me standing dumbfounded. Seeing what had happened, Bert Whalley, the United trainer, put his arm around me and explained that most of the older players would not be there next season and that the whole club would be reorganised on the basis of a strong youth policy. Only exceptional youngsters would even be considered. I replied that I was a similar age to Dennis Violet, Roger Bryne, Don Gibson, and others. "Yes," he said, "but they have been here some years and have been groomed the right way." "You are good," Bert said, "but not good enough, and the standard of player we are seeking is similar to the lad sitting over there in the corner of the dressing room." He turned out to be Duncan Edwards, and that was the beginning of the Busby Babes. I left Old Trafford feeling rejected and inadequate, and for a time my confidence dipped; served me right for being such a big head! Years later I related the story personally to Matt Busby who well remembered the period of change which transformed his club into a soccer world power.

It was never my ambition to turn professional, and I realised that without full time training and total dedication, I had gone as far as I could in top flight football.

It was also time for me to pay greater attention to my business career. I worked extremely hard with Barrow Platt, but felt uncertain about general prospects. In Spring 1952, matters came to a head when they offered me a directorship and at the same time Harry Black was making overtures for me to join him. My options were either to be tied down with security by my present employer, or to take a chance with a small concern where I could develop my own ideas and possibly create my own future. One day I believed that I would form my own company, but at the same time I needed more experience and know-how. In this connection, the textile trade was run by the Jewish fraternity, and what better way to extend my knowledge about the opposition than to work and live in their world.

Doris and I were now engaged to be married, and although some risk was involved, she supported my decision to join H Black (Textiles) Ltd where both Harry and his partner, Sonny Morris, were well known in Jewish circles. My resignation at Barrow Platt was accepted reluctantly, and I went underground to work in the cellar in St James Street in June 1952, signing a three-year contact for fourteen pounds per week and one and a quarter percent commission on all the sales I established. Given the freedom to expand the company, I put together a range of designs and colours that I sold successfully throughout the country. A considerable turnover was quickly accomplished, and my income grew accordingly.

Harry Black was a remarkable, likeable character, full of charm and good humour, and we got on fine. One of his daily habits was to disappear into the toilet each morning so that he could read his newspaper in peace. To this day if I am sometimes a long time in the loo, my wife will remark, "Have you been doing a Harry Black?"

Doris and I were married in September 1953 at Holy Trinity church in Platt Fields, but unfortunately, much to the horror of the invited Blues' fans, the day we picked coincided with a City vs United derby at Maine Road, a short distance away. The teams kicked off with a loud roar, just as we were about to tie the knot, and it was difficult to concentrate on the service whenever the crowd erupted, wondering who had scored.

The reception was held in the ballroom of the Odeon cinema in Whalley Range where, some weeks earlier, we had arranged our own bar. On the previous night, we delivered the booze, much to the astonishment of the resident manager, who informed us that he did not have a wine and spirit licence. After proving that the bar had definitely been agreed, coupled with some friendly threats, he finally consented for us to go ahead, provided we kept it quiet. When Doris and I left the Odeon late afternoon for our honeymoon, everything seemed very sedate, and we were somewhat concerned at the lack of atmosphere. We received a letter from my mother a few days later which changed our minds in no uncertain manner. It appeared that Jack Crossland, who was in charge of the bar, had spiked nearly all the drinks he served to liven up the proceedings, and this had a disastrous effect. Buddy Clyne, a six-foot-plus, eighteen-stone guest, passed out, and an attempt was made to carry him down the stairs leading from the ballroom to the ground floor of the cinema. Unfortunately two of the helpers grasped his sleeves instead of his wrists and he tumbled head over heels unconscious onto the cinema queue below. The manager, who had requested peace and quiet, witnessed the incident and nearly tore his hair out with worry. There were so many other stories such as Frank, the warehouseman, who lay on his back in the gents toilet giving an impression of Al Jolson whilst male guests stepped over him to perform. It was anything but a quiet wedding!

We spent our honeymoon at the Grand Hotel in Jersey, deciding that even if it took our last penny, we would have the best. Each evening, with Doris in her first evening gown and me in my newly purchased tuxedo, we made our way to the restaurant to be greeted by a string orchestra, as if this were an everyday occurrence. After a glorious fortnight, we returned home broke, our total wealth being a pound note left under the clock at our home in Northenden. Incredibly, for the first time in my life, I discovered the next day that I had won ten pounds on a football burster, and this saw us through the next week until pay day.

6

The business at H Black (Textiles) Ltd was continuing to expand and the company was growing at a rapid rate. Consequently the soft furnishing trade began to take notice, and it was then that one of the finest gentlemen it has ever been my privilege and pleasure to meet came into my life. Rishton Catterall was the Managing Director of S A Driver and owner of a dye works in Stalybridge. He made a courtesy call at St James's Street when looking for potential customers. He suggested that we should consider woven brocades and recommended several mills who could manufacture this more expensive commodity. The idea appeared to be well worth exploring, and I set about developing a small collection from loom state cloth and, with Rishton's assistance, produced samples in various colour ways. I then visited all regular buyers, inviting their reaction and seeking advice. With their input, we launched a brand new brocade range. This generated a higher turnover, adding personal wealth for Harry, but this did not bother me, as the commission I was earning gave me a good living.

I had been welcomed into the Jewish community and by many of the colourful characters who mainly congregated in the George Street area of Central Manchester. It did not take long for me to become acquainted with their customs and various religious ways, which I came to understand and respect. Their trading skills were very much to be admired—textiles seemed to be in the blood—and it was an invaluable education for me to live and work in their world. I attended Jewish weddings, funerals, and Bar Mitzvahs, enjoyed their food, and even learned some Yiddish, sometimes reminiscing about my early childhood days in Higher Broughton.

Some of the Jewish thriftiness must have rubbed off on me. Reg, who worked for a well-known barber's shop in Oxford Street, had been cutting my hair for the previous year or so. The charge went up from two shillings and sixpence (half a crown) to two shillings and ninepence, but when it reached three shillings, enough was enough. Following some useful tips from a sympathetic Reg, I purchased a pair of authentic barber's scissors (I still have them), and I learned to use both my left and right hands, with the aid of a hand mirror, to cut my own hair and have done so ever since.

At the turn of 1955, I became suspicious that I was not being paid all I was due, and this triggered my giving serious thought to my eventual goal to form my own company. By this time, I had cemented a close relationship with Rishton Catterall, having a high regard for his integrity and knowledge. Firmly believing that I could trust him, I explained my predicament and ambitions, and he responded by advising me to first study company law, providing various books for me to digest. Each night until the early hours, I absorbed all I could; sometimes my wife would hear me talking in my sleep, mumbling my newly found knowledge. My problem was that I had little money, and if I was to raise sufficient funds from outside sources, I would have to find a way of becoming a majority shareholder within a relatively short period of time in order to gain control of the company.

Having in theory determined the Memorandum and Articles of Association for the proposed new company, what remained was a question of securing adequate working capital. In this respect, Rishton and my old boss Jack Crossland offered to put up the cash, and this gave me the security to go ahead.

The contract with my present employer was due to expire in June 1955, plus a month's notice, meaning that I had to devote all my spare time to creating a range of designs and colours to launch the new company for the forthcoming autumn season.

Even though I had made up my mind to leave H Black (Textiles) Ltd, I still honoured my obligation to them by working flat out five days a week, and all my planning took place during the evenings until dawn at home. It was necessary for me at this stage to confidentially take on board a mill with comprehensive weaving facilities, and in anticipation of the prospect of a possibly lucrative business, a producer-salesman stuck his neck out and supported me. With Rishton providing dyed samples, I accumulated a collection of six designs, ready for the off.

May 1955 arrived, and, having concrete proof that a substantial amount of my commission had been withheld, I informed Harry Black that I intended to resign forthwith. In consultation with his partner, he said that he was going to hold me to my contract and I would not be free until the end of July. I reacted by saying that I would tear up the evidence I had of his withholding my commission if he tore up the contract, and this resulted in my immediate release. This happened on the Thursday before Whit Friday, which was then the start of a bank holiday weekend. Harry drove up to Glasgow on the following Monday to visit all the major Scottish customers. Ethically, I had not informed any of the buyers of my plans, but wherever he went, they asked, "Where is Eric? We only want to deal with him," and Harry returned home dejected, suffering a fruitless journey.

I was now free to negotiate, and I telephoned all my important contacts advising them of my plans, and it was gratifying to hear that, without exception, they would all grant me the opportunity of considering my ideas as soon as they were available.

The name of the new company was E Hughes & Co. (Textiles) Ltd, and I now needed a business address. After looking around, I settled on a third floor office at the back of Asia House in Princess Street. Most of the buildings in the area were a throw back to the prosperous era of the British overseas textiles trade and were named after world markets, such as India House, Bermuda House, Africa House and so forth. All were huge with high ceilings and two low level packing cellars. Today, most have been converted to apartments and hotels. The purpose of renting at Asia House was the availability of warehouse space when required.

I bought adequate second hand furniture from Withy Grove but had no telephone, so I kept a bag of pennies to make calls from an outside kiosk at the nearby Whitworth Street post office. By coincidence, it was exactly opposite to the address where I had first started work some twelve years ago. My budget was down to ten pounds, and if I was to distemper the walls of the office, it would cost five pounds, but to decorate with wallpaper the whole amount would be absorbed. Customers could feel sorry for me with painted walls, but could think I was making too much profit with the more elaborate look. After thinking it over, I decided on the latter, which would make a greater visual impression and convey an air of confidence, and that was that.

Doris was pregnant at the time, and we managed a cheap holiday in Devon with the knowledge that for the first time in my life, I was virtually unemployed.

The company was incorporated in July 1955, and from the nominal capital, each director, Rishton, Jack, and myself, were allocated five hundred ordinary (voting) shares each. In my contract, I received a basic salary and one half per cent commission, with an option for me to buy the remaining two thousand five hundred ordinary shares. It seemed an impossible task for me to earn enough to accomplish this quickly on such terms, but within a year I had achieved enough turnover to buy the shares and take control of the company. I then promised Rishton and Jack that I would always look after them in return for their faith in me and did just that, but did not believe at the time they would both live into their nineties.

The whole future of the company depended on the trade reaction to the new range I had developed, which I had now assembled in sample form. I telephoned the top wholesale buyer in Scotland for an appointment, and he informed me that he was coming to Manchester very shortly and was prepared to look at and consider the designs then. He was staying at what was the Grand Hotel in Aytoun Street and would see me there upon arrival from Glasgow for an evening meeting. With the samples wrapped in brown paper and with my heart in my mouth, leaving an anxious wife at home, I boarded the local bus to take me into town. The buyer greeted me in the reception area and invited me to the privacy of his bedroom, requesting me to display the samples on a deep purple bedspread, which did not sit well with coloured brocades. I did my stuff, and after I had finished showing the range there was total silence for an unbearable period, only to be broken from time to time by the buyer exclaiming, "Aye," silence, "Aye," silence, "Aye," and silence again. Then, to my immense relief, he took out his order book and bought the whole collection in depth. I returned home on a late night bus and could not wait to tell Doris the good news, which proved to be a significant turning point in our lives.

The following day I organised a weaving and dyeing programme and set about on a whirlwind tour of the UK by rail, bus, and shanks's pony and, happily, wherever I called the response to the range was terrific. Armed with a good sized order book, I then had to concentrate on deliveries. I had no storage facilities yet, but I acquired space in a warehouse located at the dye works in Stalybridge. As I had no car, I frequently caught the early morning bus and then spent the day sorting orders from the finished stock and arranging for carriers to collect and deliver direct to the customers.

It was now time to consider engaging staff, and I decided initially that a secretary with comprehensive ability and someone to assist in packing and despatch would be the priority. A wise old friend in the trade, Bill Stott, advised me not to take on a young or attractive woman because, although my marriage was sound and very happy, I could be working long hours, and it was natural for a female to become suspicious of her spouse returning home late each night. With this in mind, he knew of a spinster in her early forties looking for a job, and she possessed top qualifications in shorthand, typing, and bookkeeping. After an interview with this rather mousy but pleasant person, she became the first on my payroll and proved to be invaluable during the early days of the company. She stayed with me for a good number of years, but against character was caught making love in a bubble car in Granby Row one lunchtime and resigned out of embarrassment, although I was loathe to let her go. I heard that business was not great with Harry Black and offered Frank, a hard working, conscientious warehouseman, a job and he loyally stayed with me for many years. I then negotiated extra office space, installed telephones, and rented an adjacent warehouse, but continued to use Stalybridge for bulk deliveries.

Unfortunately, H Black (Textiles) Ltd went into liquidation, and although I had no cause to feel guilty, I was very sorry for Harry and still remember him to this day for his charm and colourful personality. Shortly afterwards, I was walking down Princess Street to my office, when coming towards me were three of the most powerful and renowned

Jewish businessmen in Manchester. For a moment I considered crossing the street, then I thought, "What the hell," and met them face to face. To my surprise they warmly greeted me with *mazel tov* and wished me well, adding, "Eric, you are more Jewish than a Jew," a fine compliment indeed.

7

Months flew by, and on 14 November 1955, Doris gave birth to a lovely baby girl, Lisa Anne, at Withington hospital. Visiting was restricted to a limited period in the evening, and having been delayed in the office, I was horrified to find that all buses had been cancelled due to heavy fog. So I set out on foot walking as quickly as I could, but arrived too late at the hospital and was not allowed in the ward. I hung around with my Pagliacci face, persuading one of the nurses to let me in and spent a few precious moments with mother and daughter.

After a few days, we settled in our treasured, small, semi-detached house in Northenden with Rusty the cat, where we spent four-and-a-half happy years before moving to Brooklands on 7 December 1957. We moved on a wet winter's night, with Doris holding Lisa on one arm and Rusty on the other. The front door had become stuck with wet paint and we had to break the window to force our way in, then the light fuses blew. Even so, seven has always been my lucky number, and we could not have chosen a better home. We are still very fortunate and content to be there to this day. My mother and father had only known backyards leading to narrow entries; to have a house with a garden would have been beyond their wildest dreams. To make their dream come true, we suggested that they move from the terraced house in Moss Side, where I lived until I was twenty-four, to the semi-detached in Northenden where they could enjoy their old age together in a much improved environment. It meant taking on two mortgages, but I felt I was repaying some of the sacrifices my parents had made when I was young.

I had now returned to amateur football and became player/coach at North Withington, my first club. Over the years we graduated from a low position in the South Manchester and Wythenshawe League to champions of the Lancashire and Cheshire League and won many honours.

Meanwhile Manchester City had reached the 1955 Cup Final but, after being beaten by Newcastle, they returned to Wembley the following year. I managed to obtain three tickets, which was very pleasing, because it meant I could take my father after he had supported the Blues for over thirty years. But there was a problem: all the rail and bus transports were fully booked. A few weeks earlier, I had purchased the first company car, still had to pass my driving test, and was very much a novice. Even so, with my brother-in-law, Bill, as the front passenger and my Father in the back we set out on a nerve-racking journey to London with 'L' plates firmly attached to the car. It was quite an experience, particularly in the nightmarish Wembley traffic, and I must have given Bill some scary moments. However, we got there and back safely to celebrate a City victory over Birmingham. Two of the players I had trained with in my early days at Maine Road, Dave Ewing and Bert Trautmann, played starring roles.

In 1957 I registered a separate export company to undertake overseas trade with the tax benefits available at the time and incorporated Eire into this category. I had been trading successfully in Northern Ireland, and my agent, George Holland, recommended that I should have a go across the border, although there appeared to be licence restrictions. George was a handsome giant of a man with a great awareness. When I first met him he was a bachelor and had been brought up by the Plymouth Brethren. His social activities had been totally curtailed until he was twenty-one years old, then the floodgates opened. He was irresistible to women, and when he came of age, he certainly made up for lost time in no uncertain manner.

Before my initial visit to Dublin, Jack Crossland said, "Whatever you do, claim you are Catholic or you will not get any business," and sure enough, on my very first call I met Ken Johnstone, who asked me if I was Catholic. I thought about it and replied, "No I am not Catholic, but I respect your religion and I hope you will respect mine." "Thank God," he said, "there are so many Englishmen coming over here lying about their religion to get orders. I like your honesty; come and have a Guinness with me."

Tom Ivory was an agent whom George knew, and at the time, he was just starting out. On our first meeting, I had to display my samples on a toilet seat in a whitewashed outbuilding at the back of his father's shop. Tom eventually rose high in Dublin society, and in the early days we worked tremendously hard together, sometimes in an unorthodox fashion, and developed a substantial turnover. To achieve this, I had to make regular visits to Eire and got to love the Irish ways, which seemed to rub off on me and add to my own personality.

Ken Johnstone was the first buyer I encountered in Dublin. He was a huge, tough man, as straight as a die and kept himself fit by running the beaches in the south of Ireland. He became a regular customer, and in Spring 1958, he placed a large order for shipment in June, which was promptly dispatched. Shortly afterwards, however, he telephoned asking if I would cancel, and I explained that the goods had already left, but if he wished I would contact the shipping company and try to divert the consignment before arrival at his warehouse. "Forget it," he retorted and hung up the receiver.

On 8 June 1958, after three weeks of waiting, Doris gave birth to our son, Stephen John, and on this occasion I was determined not to be late for the magical moment of seeing mother and son for the first time. I was about to close my office when the door burst open and Ken appeared, took off his jacket, brandished his fists like bunches of bananas and said, "Put 'em up." Apparently he had been seething since his request for cancellation and was determined to sort me out. Calming him down, I told him that I did not tell lies and the situation had been genuine. With the clock ticking he invited me out for a drink and said that bygones would be bygones. I told him that much as I would like to join him, having been given the blessing of a son born earlier in the day I had to get to the nursing home. "A fine story," he said, "Another Hughes' fairy tale," and with that he abruptly departed.

The years passed; his account had been virtually closed, and one evening Tom and I joined the England and Irish football teams for a drink in the Gresham Hotel in Dublin. Ken was there and gave me a hug, greeting me like a long-lost brother. After a while, I had to leave the party for a brief period to telephone home, and when I returned, there were at least seven whiskies lined up along the bar. Knowing I was not a heavy drinker and with a twinkle in his eye, Ken said, "Down those and we may be able to do business again." Getting Tom to distract Ken, I went through the motions of drinking, but discreetly poured the glasses into a conveniently placed plant pot on the floor at the end of the bar. The ploy worked, and he said, "I like a man who can take a drink, come and see me tomorrow."

The textile trade was changing dramatically, and the wholesale world was finding it extremely difficult due to the growth of large retail groups who had the power to buy direct from suppliers. To counter this I felt that if certain wholesale companies could offer exclusive merchandise at highly competitive rates, they would still attract business. So in 1960, I invited four of the top concerns in the UK to consider the possibility of forming a joint limited company for the purpose of bulk buying, with E Hughes (Textiles) Ltd acting as coordinator.

The Co-operative Wholesale Society could sell to their own stores in England and Wales, and the Scottish Co-operative Wholesale Society likewise in their homeland, without any outside competition. Bell and Nicholson would have the selling rights to the general retail in all areas of Great Britain, with the exception of Yorkshire and the North East to be covered by Wilkinson and Warburton. This would mean that merchandise could be offered on a confined basis at keen prices, generated by the exceptional power of combined buying. The board of directors would comprise a director appointed by each of the constituent members and myself, and buying would take place by a panel consisting of a buyer from each of the relevant four companies with myself in the chair. An accumulation of members' initial requirements alone should result in bulk quantities and provide strong argument during negotiations.

The day-to-day running of the business would be undertaken by E Hughes (Textiles) Ltd, who would retain a production charge (commission) on sales and provide expert technical and marketing advice. In addition to UK manufacture, imported goods could be introduced with obvious advantages. The capital would be nominal, but unlimited finance could be drawn from the constituent members by pro forma, allowing prompt settlement of bills.

Although the inclusion of soft furnishings would be the initial objective, there was no reason why other sections could not eventually be included, organised by separate buying panels.

In February 1961, a meeting of the proposed directors and advisors was convened in the board room of E Hughes (Textiles) Ltd to give final consideration to the project. This was scheduled for 11.00 hours, and with such important, high-profiled executives around the table, I will never forget the moment when the nearby town hall clock chimed away the seconds and in a hushed atmosphere, with my stomach churning, I addressed the meeting exactly on the stroke of eleven. All points were unanimously and amicably agreed, and Amalgamated Textile Distributors Ltd was born, and the ATD logo would be employed to identify exclusive merchandise.

The first soft furnishing debate took place in May 1961 when the buyers, who were rivals in the past, had to operate as a team. It was difficult working with different personalities, but in time the formula proved to be highly successful. Regular meetings took place, and a range of designs was formulated, with production and administration controlled by my staff. Overseas visits were arranged with a representative of the buyers' panel selected by rota and myself. We targeted manufacturers in Holland, Belgium, Germany, Italy, and even Czechoslovakia with highly beneficial results.

Other sections from the constituent members were considered, such as household goods in May 1962, hosiery in January 1963 and fashions in June 1964, where the representative buyers met to consider potential trade. For over a decade, ATD was an overwhelming success, and during 1966 to 1967, approximately 2700 invoices were exchanged. However, the size of the business was occupying too much of the time of E Hughes (Textiles) Ltd for little return, mainly due to increased overheads and labour costs. The board decided to terminate the existing method of trading in April 1972.

Meanwhile, direct buying by the retail groups and large independents now monopolised the home market, and the wholesale trade were left principally to supply smaller units in rural areas.

Although I had done my best to remain loyal, orders were diminishing at a rapid rate, and I had no other alternative but to consider the retail route. Unlike many of my competitors, I could not find it in my heart to go behind the backs of those who had supported me through the years and invited all major wholesale buyers to Manchester to explain my predicament in person. I proposed starting a new company to produce separate ideas, more suited to High Street, negotiating with large customers the wholesale trade could no longer serve. Although there was obvious dismay by some, my straight approach appeared to be appreciated, and I went ahead and registered Associated Home Fabrics Ltd with the purpose of selling under the Homemaker logo.

This began a new challenge, as I had to make inroads to a totally different way of trading with a much wider potential customer base spread over a far greater area. I travelled extensively the length and breadth of the UK, meeting buyers, researching ideas, and developing a market strategy. This included the appointments of local agents with the right connections, paid on a commission basis, and in time the business became established.

8

Opposed to the conservative and traditional character of the wholesale buyer, the retail trade was full of colourful personalities who invaded Manchester at sale times, and it required both stamina and tenacity to keep up with them. The showroom at Princess Street was open all hours, followed by the offer of dinner and entertainment, generally through the night. At the time, there were clubs galore of all standards, ranging from top cabarets to strip joints in weird locations with blue comedians and hot pot suppers thrown in as a bonus. The buyers seemed to know them all, and on one occasion a few of us ended the all-night festivities with a full English breakfast at a transport café, then home to change and face another day.

Top stars were attracted to the better clubs, and a number of textile warehouses had been converted to accommodate variety acts and music where you could rub shoulders with Shirley Bassey and other such household names. Doris and I were members of the Cabin Club, part of a small sophisticated hotel in Withington, which was ideal in hosting the more refined buyers, where the owner provided a refuge for the stars free from pressure and publicity in a relaxed atmosphere. It was there that I was able to meet Tommy Cooper, Harry Secombe, Matt Monroe, and many others over a quiet drink.

Trade shows were another major feature, and I was instrumental in organising one of the first of these at the Mount Royal Hotel in Marble

Arch, London. Suppliers hired rooms and adjusted them to show their merchandise, enabling buyers, by invitation, to concentrate their time under one roof. Entertainment was thrown in with the attraction of West End theatres and clubs, and there were many interesting stories to be told. The Berners Hotel off Oxford Street eventually became the most popular venue, and more and more suppliers became involved.

On one occasion, our northern rep, Mike Smith (one of the first agents to join Associated Home Fabrics Ltd), heard that a buyer from the southwest with very strict and religious tendencies had made an appointment to call to see us. With the devil in his eyes, Mike recruited two Bunny Girls from the Playboy Club to appear at the same time to embarrass both myself and the buyer. Two glamorous girls appeared in long coats at the doorway of the showroom, followed by Mike with a huge smirk on his face, and in full sight they disrobed, revealing the celebrated low tops and fishnet tights, then adorned their bunny ears. At the time, I was with a saintly buyer, and although I hid my feelings, I was horrified at his possible reaction. I need not have worried, however, because half an hour later he had a Bunny Girl on each knee and placed a record order.

Another year we took over the ballroom at the Westbury Hotel in the stylish Mayfair district of London, and transformed this into a showroom. George Brown, the well known, charismatic cabinet minister, was staying at the hotel, and I persuaded him to call in from time to time for a drink and to meet the various buyers. Word got around and we had a full house for the remainder of the week.

One day I felt utterly exhausted and needed time to think. I asked the manager if there was somewhere I could go to relax. He suggested a small, quiet lounge on the first floor, and as I sat down, a voice bid me, "Good afternoon," and to my surprise I was looking at Audrey Hepburn, the beautiful and charming film star. We enjoyed afternoon tea together.

As time progressed the hotels were replaced by international exhibition centres in London, Birmingham, and Manchester where suppliers organised their own stands in the company of their competitors.

I continued playing soccer, but because of my business commitments, I did not have the time to maintain a high level of fitness, and as explained in my *Life in Athletics,* I hung up my boots in 1964.

My interest in Manchester City was as strong as ever, and although they were not doing very well at the time, I supported them whenever I could. The Club had reached an all time low and were languishing in the Second Division when the Chairman at the time, little Albert Alexander, whom I remembered from my Maine Road days, asked Joe Mercer to become manager, looking for a revival. Shortly afterwards, in July 1965, the front doorbell rang, and there stood a good looking giant of a man who said, "Hello, I'm Malcolm Allison. I understand that you are involved with Manchester City." Malcolm had just been appointed Assistant Manager and Coach and had moved in to the house opposite. Joe had met Malcolm, who had just left Plymouth Argyle, at Lilleshall and recognising his potential, invited him to be his number two. Although their characters were totally different, together they wrote what was to be one of the greatest periods in City's history. Joe was the wise, genial godfather and Malcolm the dynamic, headstrong coach, but the chemistry between them was awesome.

Inspired by this partnership, City won the Second Division championship by a mile and were promoted to Division One in 1966. Malcolm was a brilliant, inventive coach, full of ideas. For example, he built up body strength through weights and special exercises so a player could take a tackle in addition to making one. One of the main features of his training programme was to assemble the whole first team squad in Wythenshawe Park each Monday morning, with on-the-spot, expert advice from international athletes Derek Ibbotson, Joe Lancaster, and Danny Herman, to develop strength, endurance, and general fitness. This included running a two-mile circuit. On one occasion, Malcolm suspected that certain players were dodging and asked me to organise a spy job by including a Sale Harrier senior athlete in the sessions to detect the guilty persons.

True enough, one of the City players (I had better not mention his name) told Steve Edmunds, my spy, to hide behind a large oak tree on the first circuit, then appear on the second leg saying, "When you pass

Malcolm remember to pant and breathe hard." Having identified the player, Malcolm was able to keep his eye on him and ensure that he gave one hundred percent in the future.

We became friends. Beth, Malcolm's wife, was a similar age to Doris, and her children, David, Dawn and Mark, got on well with Lisa and Stephen. In the early days, I helped Malcolm with transport to Maine Road. As this occurred on a regular basis, it gave me the opportunity to be associated with the club once again and to see what was going on behind the scenes. This was taken further when Malcolm arranged for three season tickets close to the players' tunnel for my father, Stephen, and myself.

Malcolm was like a character from Damon Runyon and lived life to the full, enjoying nightlife, gambling, a bottle of vintage champagne, and an after-dinner cigar, but was never late for training. The players loved him, and at the time he must have been ranked in the top three coaches in the world. I certainly learned much from him and was able to transfer some of his ideas into athletics. His playing career in football prematurely ended with West Ham after losing a lung, and while he was in hospital, he was given £1000 as compensation. He put the whole amount on a horse, won, and bought into a club on Charing Cross Road, close to the HMV recording studios where he played host to some of the world's top entertainers. From there his first official coaching position took him to Cambridge University. After tremendous success, he was made an offer to join Bath City. Then after a short, remarkable career there, he moved to Plymouth Argyle.

There were so many incidents to remember during our relationship, but one I recall happened on a snowy Boxing Day when Malcolm appeared and sheepishly asked if I could drive him to the ground as he had 'mislaid' his car. This I did, and later his car was discovered on the sixth tee at Ashton on Mersey golf club, where apparently he had spent a lively Christmas celebration.

Although he could be a hard as nails, he had a heart of gold, and two memories will forever stay in my heart. When Stephen was nine, he became seriously ill from a ruptured appendix, shortly before I was going to take him to Newcastle for the First Division title decider. Instead of cheering City to victory at St James's Park, Doris and I stayed by his bedside at Wythenshawe hospital listening to the match on the radio. Malcolm knew of Stephen's condition and got the team to sign a get well card afterwards in the dressing room and brought this round the same night. We took the card, complete with mud stains, to the hospital the next day and I am sure the gesture helped Stephen's recovery. It is still one of his most treasured possessions.

It was a sickening blow when my father had to have his leg amputated, and once he was fitted with a false limb, I was able to take him to the main entrance of Maine Road and help him to his seat. The most important football occasion in Manchester is, of course, the local derby. For the City vs United home match, Malcolm arranged for my father to join the teams in the tunnel, and with captains Colin Bell holding one arm and Bobby Charlton the other, he experienced the rapturous welcome from 60,000 voices. My father cried his eyes out in a never-to-be-forgotten moment, and I will always be grateful to Malcolm for his understanding and kindness.

Following the First Division championship in 1968, City went on to win the FA Cup in 1969 and the European Cup Winners Cup in 1970.

My textile company had continued to develop in all sections, including the addition of a factory to manufacture made-up goods. We now occupied four floors at Asia House, and turnover was spread over limited wholesale trade, the ever growing retail business, and the export market in such countries as Australia, New Zealand, and the Far East.

However, in 1973, along with all other tenants, we were given notice to quit Asia House. For some time we had become dissatisfied with the general service provided by the owners, principally poor hoist and loading facilities, which seriously affected incoming and outgoing goods. Also the ever-increasing traffic problem in central Manchester made it impossible for collection and deliveries, with restless lorry drivers waiting for hours in vain. Ken Colquhoun, our accountant, advised that although the company was doing well, we had no fixed assets, and that owning our own building would be a huge advantage.

After months of searching, we decided that a location in South Manchester would be ideal and acquired a site close to the M56 motorway and near the airport. A purpose-built building, which we christened Hyline House, was designed and erected. This included the benefit of working from one ground level, opposed to operating from four separate floors at Asia House. After a number of confrontations with the property developer, in 1975 we moved in lock, stock and barrel.

Mother and Father Wedding Day

Eric Age 6 Years

Eric With Jack Crossland

Eric RAF

Doris Age 19 Years

Eric With Rover

Eric and Doris Honeymoon in Jersey

North Withington Team Eric Player-Coach (Eric With Ball)

Doris With Young Family Lisa and Stephen

Eric and Doris 1977 West Indies

Eric 1997 Receiving Sir Matt Busby Lifetime Achievement Award
(By Courtesy of Manchester Evening News)

Doris (right) and Leora 1997 United After 55 years

Eric and Doris 2008

9

A friend of mine, David Spurway, a director of a well-known net manufacturer, decided to take over an established selling agency in South Africa and emigrated there to begin a new life. Our speciality in brocades and weaves was in demand, and he suggested that he could sell on our behalf on a commission basis. Furthermore, he recommended that I should go out there once he had settled down to provide personal support. Because the prospects appeared to be good, I set out in January 1972 with a bag of samples in the hope of much needed orders.

David had offices in Johannesburg, Durban, and Cape Town and had arranged for me to make the grand tour. The nature of the agency was colonial and the connections were traditional accounts, mostly with the white population. I did not like apartheid, which meant, at that particular time, segregation and poor treatment of black labour. For example, David employed a man and his wife to work at his home full-time, and at the end of the week, the woman was given just a bag of sugar, which she devoured on a Friday night. The husband's treat was a few rand which he spent on drink in the city centre of Johannesburg, a dangerous place at weekends where members of the various tribes recalled their ancestral hatred and set about each other in drunken brawls.

South Africa was a fascinating country, and I enjoyed the experience, but overall I was disappointed with the business received, which just about covered expenses. Before I left, Lenny Abelheim, a buyer from one of the private wholesalers, invited me for a drink to ask how I had got on. He stated that if I was to be successful, I would have to work through agents who could reach the mass market, which included trade to the black, coloured, and Asian communities. He paid me a compliment by saying that he liked my way of thinking, and he believed that the products I was carrying could sell if I dealt with the right customers. If I was interested, he knew of two top-class, hard-working agents, one who personally covered Johannesburg, Durban, and Bloemfontein, and the other a world famous character to whom he was related who operated in the Cape. I gave the matter considerable thought and decided that the colonial route would not be the best option and eventually took up Lenny's offer.

Having terminated the arrangement with David, I negotiated terms with Stephen Boyer in Johannesburg and Nathan Shapiro in Cape Town and agreed to return for a personal visit.

Meanwhile I had been investigating the possibility of trading with other African nations and had appointed an agent in Kenya. S.G. Carrington Agencies had been initiated by an Englishman some years ago who had handed down the company on his retirement to Wakefield Wanjohi, his top black salesman. While planning my trip to South Africa I discovered there was a stop en route in Nairobi during the early hours of the morning, so I booked my British Airways flight allowing for a twenty-four hour stay to review the market. I arranged for a hotel room so I could freshen myself up, giving me a full working day before boarding the night flight to Johannesburg.

Wakefield Wanjohi agreed to meet me at the airport, but unfortunately we arrived late, and as I was anxious to let him know I was there, I ignored passport control. Looking out from the barrier on a sea of black faces, all of which seemed to be the same, I called out, "Wanjohi!" A hand shot up, and I waved to acknowledge my presence. It was then that I felt a sharp pain in my shoulder, and turning around I confronted a small, black army officer covered in braid and medals who had struck me with his cane. He, quite rightly, told me that I had no business to be there, but when he repeated the blow I snatched the cane from his hand and broke it in two. The little dictator then summoned several policemen with the intention of arresting me, but just at that moment the captain of the BA jumbo passed by and enquired as to what the fuss was all about. When I explained, he told the obnoxious little man to release me or he would report to the authorities that he had struck me first, and I made a hasty exit.

I managed a couple of hours sleep then enjoyed a good day's business, opening with all the top accounts in Nairobi before boarding my onward flight. One thing I will remember during my brief stay is that wherever I went, in every street and building, either a statue had been erected or a picture displayed of Jomo Kenyatta, the President at the time and famous for the Mau Mau uprising.

Stephen Boyer met me at the airport in Johannesburg and had booked me in at the Carlton Hotel, contrary to the more economical accommodation I had endured on my last trip. Both his and Nathan Shapiro's outlooks were totally different, as they believed that staying at the best hotels reflected a more successful image.

Upon my arrival at the hotel the place was throbbing with excitement with crowds of people, television, film, and radio crews. This was the first time in the Republic's history that an Asian had married a black woman whose relatives had never before left their homeland in the bush. The modern world was too much for some of the confused guests, and women in highly coloured robes were screaming with fright when having to travel up the moving escalator from the lobby.

The trip began with a bang when Stephen informed me that he had arranged for an appointment the following Sunday morning, 7.30 a.m., at his office, and right on time three vans appeared from which emerged a dozen Indians whom I greeted one by one. Over the Coca Cola provided, I was invited to present my range, and each buyer made his own separate choice. This was then coordinated by the leader of the party and, in due course, a bulk order was placed that would be shipped in one consignment, then divided upon arrival according to individual selection. I joined Stephen and his wife for lunch, and we got to know each other while planning an ambitious sales programme.

The contacts were there, including OK Bazaars, one of the country's major accounts, and in two days I sold more than the previous visit put together. It was a question of being up at dawn, working an action-packed day, then entertaining at night where I was accepted into the Johannesburg social circles.

We flew to Bloemfontein for the day where it was very different dealing with the hard, arrogant Boers. I travelled on my own to stay in Durban over the weekend, with Stephen proposing to join me on Monday morning. In a land of many climates, Durban is below sea level and the humidity was overbearing. On a Saturday morning, I toured Zulu land and ran some of the beaches, but on Sunday one of the worst rain storms ever hit the city, and cars were literally floating down the streets. Stephen managed to land, we completed a hard day's work, and we left on the last flight before the area was marooned.

Leaving for Cape Town began one of the most amazing times of my life. Because I had heard so much about Nathan Shapiro, I was a little uncertain what to expect. In my mind, I had visualised someone tall, good looking, with an imposing presence, but when there was a tap on my shoulder I turned, surprised to see a small, portly, Jewish gentleman with a slightly turned eye who said, "Are you Eric, I'm Nathan." This was my first meeting with the best salesman I would ever know.

We retired to the car park, and sitting in his car he grilled me on my background and interests. Nathan seemed delighted to learn of my sporting activities, in particular that of my involvement with Manchester City, and although I explained I had not played at first team level, he did not seem to mind. When leaving the airport, he asked me if I would mind accompanying him to his sister's home on the way to the hotel. She lived on the slope of Table Mountain, and she was heavily pregnant. Nathan was concerned about her well-being. As we approached the area, we were dismayed to see that the mountain side was on fire, with a following wind taking the flames towards the house we were visiting. Nathan's sister was in a terrible state and with her young daughter had collected her most precious valuables ready for evacuation. I carried her outside with Nathan following clutching the child and valuables, but just after we passed through the front garden miraculously the wind changed direction and we were safe.

Eventually I was checked in at the President's Hotel on First Beach, ready to begin a memorable working week.

The most important account in the Cape was Ackermans, and on my last visit I could not even get an appointment there. However, this was the first call on the agenda, and because Nathan was treated like a god, we strolled through to the executive offices, where he introduced me to the buyer, then left me to do my stuff. I took what I considered to be a good order, but when Nathan returned he asked the buyer what he had bought, and much to my amazement tore up the order saying, "Now, give Eric a decent order." This was three times the volume and enough to keep a weaving shed busy for some months. It appeared that when Nathan had left us earlier, he had called on his friend who happened to be the president of the company and whose life he had once saved from a house fire, as well as rescuing his safe containing an absolute fortune. I was beginning to realise that all the stories I had heard about Nathan were true, and it was a privilege to work with such a legend.

Upon departing from Ackermans, he invited the buyer to a Farewell to Eric barbeque at the end of the week and mentioned that I had 'starred for Manchester City in the First Division'. As the week progressed, with one call after another, I graduated to the captaincy of City, was a full England international, and had scored a hat trick at Wembley. I got past blushing, accepted my celebrity role, and was welcomed around town, which in turn resulted in plenty of business.

Taking his leave one evening, Nathan said, "Tomorrow I am really going to test you out." There was a huge warehouse on the outskirts of Cape Town which mainly dealt with the coloured population. Nathan told me that if I played my cards right, we could take a large order. To make this possible, I had to do exactly what he told me, even though no one had yet had the guts to follow his advice. This was okay with me, and early the next day we arrived ready for action at a massive, gloomy building piled high with bales of cloth and rolls of fabric.

Nathan said that the buyer I was going to meet was the ugliest woman ever, but "I want you to tell her that she is beautiful. Also she is the world's worst cook and I want you to tell her that she makes a wonderful meal." This seemed unreal, but as I had complete belief in Nathan's judgment, I agreed to do what he asked. It was then zero hour, and out of the gloom came the owner. She had little, watery eyes, a pallid face covered with warts, and she wore a long cardigan down to her bony knees. Nathan nudged me and said, "Go ahead," and after the introduction, with sweaty palms and a racing heart, I gulped, took a deep breath, and heard myself say, "I am very pleased to meet you Miss Davis, I think you are very beautiful." "Thank you," she replied, then I added, "I understand you are a wonderful cook and maybe one day I could have the privilege of sampling your skills." "Thank you," she said again. We then got down to business, an excellent order was placed, and on departure the lady said, "Eric, I know I am ugly, and I know I cannot cook, but your kind words meant so much to me, thank you again." Once more Nathan was right, what a man!

Shortly after I arrived in South Africa, I was given a ticket in the directors' box for the National Cup Final to be held in Cape Town during my stay. The local soccer world at that time was graced by Johnnie Haynes and Frank Lord, who had done so much to lift the image of the sport, and the match was a sell out. Upon learning of this, Nathan said, "My son has always wanted to sit in the directors' box, why don't you allow him to do so and join me and my friends in the main stand?" I could not refuse, but sensed he had something up his sleeve. True enough, when we appeared at the top of the stand the whole crowd stood up as one, applauded and shouted my name. From the corner of my eye I could see the satisfied smirk on Nathan's face.

After one of the most exhausting weeks of my life I had reserved the Friday afternoon before leaving just to relax and enjoy the beach and sunshine. When Nathan heard of my plan, he told me to forget it, as he wanted a favour from me, but did not disclose what it was to be. I was to appear at his office just after lunch, and when I did so, I was introduced to eight overweight millionaires who were all connected with the diamond trade. Nathan announced, "This is Eric, a top athletic coach, and he is going to instruct you on how to lose weight and get fit." For an hour or so I lectured on the benefits of diet and exercise, emphasising that a gradual transformation would be necessary with the latter as an abrupt change in habits could result in a possible heart attack. After suggesting they all meet me on First Beach the following Saturday morning, I hurried to get ready for the barbeque being held in my honour with all the buyers and their wives in attendance.

My pupils turned up on time, wearing the most expensive tracksuits imaginable. I borrowed a car, worked out a mile circuit, and told my athletes to jog just ten metres, then walk the rest of the course. This was to take place each day for a week, and then increase to twenty metres and so on until the whole mile was completed. So was the Weightwatchers Club of the Cape born, and for years afterwards I received a greeting card from them.

Upon my brief return to Johannesburg I thanked Lenny Abelheim personally for his help and for making my visit so successful, then boarded a flight for home.

I was to see Lenny and his wife on regular visits to the UK, and although he travelled the world, he genuinely believed that his next flight would be his last. He would always telephone Hannah, his wife, before boarding to say goodbye, convinced that he would never speak to her again. On one homeward flight he sent a message to the captain that he was going to die and this resulted in the aircraft landing in an Arab state to set him down for medical attention. Poor Lenny was abandoned for a number of days in a country hostile to Jews before he could continue on his journey.

The trade to South Africa was short-lived, as the next year government restrictions were imposed making importation practically impossible.

Lisa, age sixteen by this time, was studying at Manchester High with her eye on a medical career. Stephen, then thirteen, was doing well at Sale Grammar, especially in art. Both ran middle distance and had appeared in the All England and National Cross Country Championships, competing for both school and club. Doris, as ever, gave me her love and understanding, supporting me whatever the circumstances.

10

The loss of the South African market was a blow, but out of the blue another overseas opportunity emerged. One morning the telephone rang in my office and a gentleman by the name of John Wilford introduced himself, saying that he was with K Funduklian & Co Ltd. This was a long established textile merchant known to me as an office boy when collecting samples for the Allied National Corporation. He asked if he could call and bring along Mr Vahl Funduklian to discuss a business possibility, following a recommendation made by the Manchester Chamber of Commerce.

We met the day after, when it was explained that they now earned a living from long standing connections in the West Indies. Mr Vahl Funduklian, a prominent figure in Rugby Union, was originally Armenian, but nationalised as British, and the last remaining survivor of the Funduklian family, which dated back to early Bible days. He was approaching eighty years and wore a Crombie overcoat he had purchased in 1925, John Wilford being about ten years his junior. It would appear that John had travelled the West Indies for many years, making his first trip on a banana boat, and visited the various islands annually with a bag of samples from which he obtained orders for shipment after his return.

Whenever possible, it was an advantage for him to offer exclusive merchandise, and he enquired if we were interested in supplying them on that basis. Although at the time I was unaware of the market potential, there was nothing to lose, and I agreed to support these two lovely old gentlemen.

John duly set off early January to cover Guyana, Barbados, Trinidad, Jamaica, and the Bahamas and surprised me with the overall volume he had booked when he landed back in this country.

This became a yearly exercise until one day, late 1974, John phoned to see if he and Mr Funduklian could pop in for a coffee. They told me that they were getting too old to continue and had to call it a day. I exclaimed, "What a shame after all these years!" I thanked them for the business placed and wished them well. The next day the phone rang once more, with John asking if I would be in and if they could call again. I replied that they were always welcome, wondering at the same time the purpose of the visit. Mr Funduklian soon got to the point, saying that both he and John had been moved by my kind words and how much they had appreciated the support given in recent years. He then added that they would like to make me a gift of the company and its connections, provided:

(1) that we retained the name of K Funduklian & Company Limited;

(2) that we gave 'young' John (now 73 years) a job to provide him with some form of income; and

(3) that I personally went out to the West Indies to maintain the business.

At the time we were badly in need of orders, so I agreed to his conditions and quickly attended to the necessary legal matters.

In 1975 arrangements were made for John and his wife Kath to make a farewell tour of the islands and for me to join him in Barbados to learn the ropes.

Guyana was discounted due to the dubious political situation and the appalling crime rate generated by an extreme state of poverty. A doctor friend of John's had attended a conference there some months previous and had taken his wife with him. One day, he was kept late and arranged for his wife to return to their hotel by taxi. Upon arrival she rolled down the window, placed her hand outside and had it instantly severed by a desperate robber with a machete who made off with her rings still on her fingers.

Barbados, one of the most literate countries in the world, could not have been more different, with its English traditions, yacht clubs, plush hotels, and, of course, its love for cricket. Bridgetown was the centre of activity, and we were represented by Geddes Grant, a long standing and famous trading company who acted as our agents. I was welcomed at the airport by Tony Lawless, who managed our account in the company of John and Kath, and first experienced the warm, subtropical breezes that greeted me. Tony, a huge bear of a man with a perpetual twinkle in his eye and a dry sense of humour, was well known on the island for his whimsical character and knowledge of textiles, being acquainted with all the right people.

Geddes Grant arranged for our accommodations at the Ocean View, a small private hotel akin to something from a Somerset Maugham novel, with old, friendly and courteous black waiters wearing white gloves. The hotel was actually situated on a small beach, with flying fish playing in the nearby Caribbean sea and wonderful sunsets to accompany an evening drink, locally described as a 'Sundowner'. John's popularity was apparent, and we booked orders with all the major accounts before taking off for Trinidad, our next port of call.

From the sophistication of Barbados, we entered the world of one of the most cosmopolitan nations on the planet with dusty streets, masses of people, and loud music everywhere. The main revenue of Trinidad came from oil, pitch, sugar, and citrus fruit, and no business trip should ever be arranged around Carnival time. The whole population prepares for this weeks in advance; no work is done during Carnival; and it takes a full week to recover. Our hotel was adjacent to the Savannah where ten cricket matches could take place at the same time and which also boasted a race track.

Errol Shim, our agent, was a youthful looking Chinaman who had been a water polo international and had swum from Trinidad to Tobago. He was quiet, thoughtful, and well trusted, and together we sat down to map out a programme. The hustle and bustle of Port of Spain, the capital, suited me fine, and here I was to experience one of the most amazing few days of my selling career, after I had been warned that I would have to adapt to the many different personalities from mixed nationalities. For example, the Syrians were very aggressive both verbally and physically, and I had to remain strong and behave similarly, whereas the true Trinidadians were polite and good mannered and had to be treated with respect. One Jewish customer actually cried when I gave him prices, and an Indian buyer asked us to wait in the rear of his store without air conditioning. After we had been roasted sufficiently, he asked to see samples, hoping our resistance would be low enough for us to agree counter offers. I had to bow continually to the Chinese, but there was no doubt in my mind that in Port of Spain, the power was with the Syrians, who were in fierce competition with each other, and I spent a lot of time studying their habits and techniques.

The most beneficial part of the trip was the day we spent on the other side of the island in San Fernando, which reminded me of a Wild West town. This was mostly populated by Indians who enjoyed the benefit of its oil refineries, and here we picked up record orders.

It was surprising that 'Lord John', as he was known, had done little entertaining over the years, and I used the excuse of his retirement to invite buyers out to get to know them better. On our last night in Trinidad, I took John, Kath, and Errol to the top floor of the Holiday Inn where the world famous jazz pianist Dennis de Souza was playing. After a few drinks, a tall, dark South American sea captain with film star looks asked Kath for a dance. She was very flattered, so she accepted, and during the evening he never left her side. I could see that John was getting more and more agitated and hot under the collar with jealousy, and as there was such an age difference, I suggested that Kath ask the good-looking Romeo why he was so infatuated. His answer completely deflated Kath as he replied, "Because you remind me of my mother," and this, needless to say, did little for her ego.

My conclusion after leaving Trinidad was that we were dealing with too many customers who were price-cutting each other, and I felt that a much larger turnover could be achieved by consolidating trade.

The next stop was Jamaica, which was undergoing political unrest because it had established relations with Cuba by introducing socialistic policies. It appeared that all orders taken would be subject to confirmation by the government, as rigid control on all imports had been enforced. Even so, appointments had been made by our agent

Edward Khan with old, established customers and if you don't try, you don't succeed.

Our accommodation was in a country club, about a mile from the centre of Kingston, where we were housed in little cabins protected by barbwire, with security guards everywhere.

We were treated with courtesy and respect by all buyers, who were old friends of John, and although orders were placed, I was not too optimistic they would be approved in full by the authorities. The state of the country worried me, but at least I had acquired knowledge of the market and would know my way around should I wish to return.

The final stage of the tour was in Nassau in the Bahamas, with its American way of life in total contrast to the gloom and strife of Jamaica. Cora Carey, our agent, was a flamboyant, imposing woman and a powerful figure in the local community, with many irons in the fire. Cora bought me my first ever piña colada and enlightened me with all the latest news, not least how I should relate to the customers. Her advice was first rate, and together we developed a good working relationship that resulted in orders beyond expectations.

We returned home, from what John and Kath described as their best trip ever, and John made his commercial base at a desk in the corner of the production office at Hyline House. From there he acted as our West Indies consultant, giving advice and attending to licence problems and other related matters. He received a commission on all ongoing sales relevant to the countries we had visited, this being my way of fulfilling the promise to provide an income for young John.

During the ensuing year I spent time developing ideas and colours to suit West Indian taste, and in 1976 left the cold January weather behind to arrive in Barbados on the start of my first solo tour. My aim was to combine the prestige and goodwill that John had created over the years with my own personality and business techniques, while at the same time earning the respect of the agents and buyers alike.

After a good day in Bridgetown, I was invited onto the maiden voyage of the Jolly Roger, a pirate ship sailing off the nearby coast line, the guest list including VIPs from the island, politicians, celebrities, film stars, and millionaires. We were greeted by the captain, who informed us that barrels of rum were freely available on all decks, and that at the end of the festivities we would have one of two options, to either walk off or be carried off. Food was served from barbeques, and live music was provided by the Merry Men, a world famous group who were extremely popular in America and Canada. As the evening progressed, the scenes were incredible, with guests diving overboard, fully clothed, to be rescued by crew members. Having a busy programme the following day, I was careful, without being too unsociable, but even so as I walked off in the early hours, I was somewhat worse for wear. The trip went well, and I cemented relationships, but it was obvious that to get into the heart of business, I had to become more involved in local society.

I had no doubt that Trinidad had the greatest potential, and to expand turnover I had to change the existing sales policy to create a new image in keeping with the younger generation of Syrians who monopolised trade in Port of Spain, the capital.

The first step was to establish a more prestigious base, and I reserved a room in the Hilton Hotel, the place to be. The Hilton was nicknamed 'Upstairs' and 'Downstairs' as, being built on a hill: instead of taking the lift up from reception to your room, you travelled down.

Through Errol Shim, I let it be known that I intended to consolidate trade and arranged a meeting at the hotel between all the top Syrian buyers. This caused quite a stir, as most of them rarely spoke to each other because of the fierce rivalry between the families. However, the response was good, and talking face to face, I explained that in the past we had been dealing with too many customers, which had created unnecessary competition and, in some instances, price cutting. My proposal was to limit distribution so each buyer could secure fair prices on designs that would not be flogged around. The reaction was very favourable, and I picked up record business with this new strategy.

I then boarded a 747 bound for Jamaica, where on arrival all passengers and crew were escorted into a large hall and told to stay there. After a while the British Consulate appeared and explained that a civil war was expected, and because of riots, Kingston was out of bounds. We were all grounded and for safety confined to the Sheraton Hotel, just outside the city, and were to remain there until the trouble had passed. I had come a long way to get business and, rightly or wrongly, not to be outdone, I sneaked out of the hotel to keep appointments.

The atmosphere in Kingston was horrific, with bodies lying in the streets and chaos everywhere, and families were rubbing each other out dependent on the political party they supported. Although the buyers thought I was mad even to be there, they appreciated my efforts and gave me every possible support.

I returned to the hotel with Edward Khan, where we had a drink by the swimming pool. He told me the price of assassinations had fallen to an all time low. To prove the point, he beckoned to someone he knew to be a hit man who quoted a mere ten pounds per person for murder, life being so cheap.

It was interesting living with and getting to know the BA captain and crew for a few days, and on the flight to Nassau, they provided champagne on my birthday.

Cora Carey was there to meet me at the airport, and we got on like a house on fire, concluding the overall trip on a high note.

11

On reflection I realised more and more the importance of social life in the West Indies, and asked Doris to join me on the 1977 visit. Our departure did not get off to a good start, as the flight was delayed because of snow. Worse still, on her first long distance flight, Doris had the misfortune to sit next to a hypochondriac who talked air disasters for the whole journey. Doris loved Barbados and its people and was enchanted with the Ocean View and its old world charm. She made a good impression when accompanying me on calls, buyers made a fuss of her and invited us out, the first step to making inroads into the close-knit Bajan society.

I had already warned Doris that Trinidad would be completely different to the quiet, colonial life in Barbados and to expect hustle, bustle, loud music, and dusty streets.

We checked in at the Hilton, but before we had time to unpack, messages were received from a number of the Syrian buyers anxious to get first sight of the new designs we had to offer. Doris appeared to like Errol Shim, with his quiet and polite personality, and we went through a sales programme for the following day.

After changing for dinner, while having a drink on the hotel's rooftop on a warm, romantic, subtropical night, we first heard 'Feelings', played by the resident orchestra, and to this day it remains one of our favourites. There could not have been a more contrasting setting when, in a bustling San Fernando store later in the week, we listened to a recording of this a second time. Roland Khan, the buyer and owner, treated us to lunch in his office, consisting of Colonel Sanders' Kentucky Fried Chicken in cartons with a roll of toilet paper to clean our greasy hands.

As in Barbados, Doris's presence with me did the trick, and we were inundated with social invitations, getting to know buyers, their wives, and their families. Music was everywhere, and our dancing background came in useful when joining in the rhythm of the calypso and other vibrant West Indian sounds.

With a sense of trepidation we caught an early morning flight to Jamaica to find the situation had worsened and quickly detected that even if orders were placed, there would be little chance of these being confirmed. Kingston was a very dangerous place to be, but we kept our appointments. We found that doors were heavily barricaded and guarded, and the buyers had guns to hand on their desks. Total depression had taken over, and it was heartbreaking to see desperate teenagers sitting in the gutters with hopeless looks on their faces and little or no future. It was obvious we had to get out quickly, and after cancelling our hotel accommodation, we bribed a taxi driver to take us to the airport. Because of the petrol shortage he demanded double if he travelled at normal speed, otherwise the journey was going to take ages by driving slowly to conserve fuel.

Luckily, we managed to get a flight to Nassau, our next destination, but we arrived in the early hours and the airport was shut down. Because no one was there to meet us, we were stranded. I had an idea where we were staying, and after hanging around the deserted airport for some time, we eventually located a taxi. As we were not expected at the hotel, there was more delay, but eventually we collapsed in our room after a long and exhausting day.

The next morning I contacted Cora Carey who, on joining us for lunch, immediately hit it off with Doris, both sharing a mutual interest in clothes and fashions. Unbelievably it *snowed* the following day for the first time ever in the Bahamas, and every available heating appliance and items of woollen clothing were sold out in a matter of hours. Thankfully this was short lived, the sunshine returned and the trip went well.

With more leisure time, Doris was able to see more of local life and was fascinated with the straw market, but after viewing the ocean bed from a glass bottomed boat felt she was "intruding on the privacy of the fishes."

One night we linked up with two Canadian couples and hired a minibus to take us to Paradise Island casino. Talk about a small world, as one of the women, who was Cheshire born and residing in Toronto at the time, had an uncle living just around the corner from our home in Brooklands. We parted company with the wives who had decided to try their luck on the slot machines while the men had a drink. Although it may seem hard to believe, each one of them scored a jackpot, and the proceeds paid for dinner and the floorshow.

Cora held a farewell dinner at her home, but her children were late arrivals after attending the premier of the first 'Rocky' film. After a short stop in Bermuda, we returned home and reflected on a very successful mission.

Doris joined me again in 1978 when we concentrated on Barbados and Trinidad to cement the relationships we had established the previous year. We planned more time in Barbados and arranged a couple of days at Sam Lord's Castle. Located on the far side of the island, this was a holiday resort named after the famous pirate who was executed in the Tower of London for his wicked deeds. We found the atmosphere totally different, being treated as tourists as opposed to being part of the community, and we were more than happy to return to work.

The sister of one of the Geddes Grant directors ran a bar and hotel called the Coconut Club, and we joined a small party for dinner and entertainment there. We were sitting at the bar when the door suddenly opened, and there stood Oliver Reed wearing just his underpants and a policeman's helmet. He had procured this in London before leaving and had stopped for a drink at every pub between the airport and the Coconut Club. Oliver was a personal friend of the owner, a woman who swore like a trooper and told dirty jokes; they were quite a couple.

Saying farewell to Barbados, we arrived in Trinidad and were welcomed by all and sundry. We mixed freely in the business circles of both Port of Spain and San Fernando.

Excitement was mounting with the near expectation of carnival. The shops had benefited from a bonanza of fabric sales, and everyone was putting finishing touches to the most amazing costumes imaginable. Just before the opening day, the whole population divides into large bands, who then sing and dance their way through the streets in a blaze of colour and spectacle, with no thought of sleep. This goes on for a whole week and it takes at least the same amount of time to recover and clean up.

One story that amused us entailed a serious corruption trial being held in Port of Spain, with a number of well known politicians in the dock. The case was in its final and critical stages, but the judge decided that proceedings would be adjourned until after the carnival, and everyone went home.

To herald the arrival of the carnival, early celebrations were held all over the island, and we were invited to a number of these. On one occasion, a large area near the docks had been cleared, a stage erected, and food and drink provided for over one thousand people who danced the mambo en masse and sang throughout the night. The atmosphere was electric, the music loud but infectious, and it took all of our stamina to keep pace. With a good order book under our belts, we used the journey home to unwind and catch up on much needed sleep.

12

Reverting to the home market, although my company had the reputation of producing something different, we were running out of fresh ideas. The managing director of a well known jacquard weaver in Blackburn knew of a world famous designer in Berlin named Willi Herman and suggested that it would be a good idea to visit his studio in Germany. I had a sound working relationship with his sales manager, Geoff Peake, and arrangements were made for us to pursue this. At the time, I had been looking at the Danish market, had provisionally appointed an agent, and had agreed to accompany him on an exploratory trip in June 1976. After a few days, Geoff would join me in Copenhagen, and from there we would fly to Berlin together.

My brief spell in Denmark was interesting and educational, but once more I was involved in a rather bizarre situation. All our business appointments were just outside the town square, and I could not understand why, after each call, we always ended up back there before we moved on. It was later that I discovered my agent's wife had a small newspaper and tobacco kiosk in the square. He believed she was having an affair, so he kept circling the kiosk over and over again checking up on her.

Our first night in Berlin was memorable and after booking in at the Kempinski hotel, Geoff, being a bit of a lad, found his way to a nearby bar famous for typical German oompah-pah music. After a few drinks and a singsong, led by Geoff bellowing out tunes from his scout days, we found ourselves in dubious company, and someone suggested that we visit a night club across town that opened late. I did not take particular notice of the surroundings at first, but gradually realised from the derelict buildings that we were in the Russian sector. In the days of the Berlin Wall this was a very dangerous place to be, and indeed only the day previous an American officer had been found stripped and dead by the Brandenburg Gate. Luckily, I was more sober than Geoff and found a taxi driver who knew his way back through the Wall's boundary. It cost us a fortune, but we eventually arrived back at the hotel in the early hours. We had just enough time to shower and get changed before we had to meet the car that would take us to the studio.

Willi Herman was a charming, intelligent, and gifted man and he invited us to address a small group of designers with our ideas. Thereafter they retired to their drawing boards and worked on sketches to be prepared that same evening for our scrutiny. After more reinforcements of black coffee and a tour of Berlin, we returned to the studio for a second session ,which comprised approving or rejecting sketches and giving licence to proceed with selected creations. Unbelievably, the designers worked through the night, and finished paintings, drawn to scale, were there for us the following morning. This exercise was repeated the day after, and we took the paintings back with us, to be applied and introduced into the British market as a new look.

Another time I joined forces with Henry Birtwistle to embark on a design research mission covering the length and breadth of Europe. Henry, a codirector of one of our principal suppliers, was a quiet and studious person in contrast to Geoff Peake, and his company would benefit from any positive ideas that might result from the trip.

We began in Brussels, moved on to Paris, and concluded in Milan and Rome, meeting designers, and checking museums and major stores. While having a farewell drink with Henry in a well known bar before he had to return home, we got into conversation with someone who represented the national music industry. He was awaiting the arrival of the express train from Zurich bringing a collection of the latest pop music to be introduced into the Italian market. Included was a song named 'Que Sera, Sera' and he asked if we knew of this. His eyes sparkled when I told him this was a tremendous hit by Doris Day and was top of the charts in the UK and many other countries. Apparently he received a commission based on circulation and was so delighted that he bought a round of drinks and organised for us to dine in a famous La Scala restaurant. It was there I learned how to eat spaghetti correctly, and by coincidence the proprietor knew a contessa in Rome who would be a good design and art contact.

I parted company with Henry and arrived in the Eternal City late on Friday afternoon. From my hotel on the Via Vento, I telephoned the Contessa, who informed me she was just leaving on holiday. However, she gave me useful information that I could pursue on the Monday, and I found myself with a free weekend to enjoy the sights. The weather was very hot, and on foot I made my way to St Paul's, the Pantheon, the Spanish Steps, and even visited the Catacombs off the Appian Way. My most memorable experience was sitting on the top steps of the Colosseum and letting my mind wander back to the ancient times of the slaves and gladiators.

Foolishly, in the heat, I ate too much fruit and the delicious frozen ices on sale everywhere to which I had become addicted. In consequence, I suffered a violent attack of the runs, and in the midst of the city was desperate to find a toilet. The nearest appeared to be in the central railway station, so I rushed through the crazy traffic, risking life and limb in my desperation to get there, only, to my horror, to be confronted with the sign *'toiletto'* down posted at each platform level. I hurtled down the staircase, covering three flights, and finally flung myself into a cubicle just in time. A madam was banging on the door, and I discovered that I was in the ladies room, but she seemed more angry that I had not left any money in the saucer when I had made my dramatic entrance. With immense relief, I sat there for some time with my head between my hands staring at the floor, and there before me was a beautiful cubic image which I traced using toilet paper and this turned out to be a very successful furnishing design.

Some time had passed since the inaugural soft furnishings show had taken place at the Mount Royal hotel in London. Professional exhibitors had taken over and in November 1976 the venue had moved to the NEC in Birmingham, where it was now regarded as an international event. Several large halls housed specially erected stands displaying suppliers' wares, and buyers roamed the aisles placing orders, taking notes and picking up current and future trends. My sales and production staff moved en bloc to the show, and joined by our agents from various parts of the country, the exercise proved to be a good marketing and bonding operation. Doris helped out on the stand and was popular for providing a cup of freshly brewed tea in contrast to the continuous flow of alcohol offered by our competitors. Lisa and Stephen were both studying at Birmingham University, and we were able to hold a family get together during our stay.

Concentration was still on piece goods, and the show presented an excellent opportunity to extend overseas trade. We had developed two outstanding fabrics that attracted plenty of attention, particularly from buyers and agents from Scandinavia, and it was there I forged links with two agents which led to a substantial turnover over the next five years.

Gunner Birkevold was from Norway, and he guaranteed business if I appointed him to represent us. I said, "Prove it," and accordingly the following day he brought two of his country's top buyers on to the stand who placed large orders with the proviso that Gunner was involved. We shook hands on the deal and I promised to accompany him later on a visit to Norway.

Bjorn Sjoberg came from Sweden and also appeared to be well connected. With the expectation of concrete business, I agreed a trial appointment with my personal support.

Thus began yet another episode in the company's history, and for the next few years, my trips would have me endure the heat of the West Indies one minute and then suffer the intense cold of Scandinavia the next; talk about blowing hot and cold.

13

Being encouraged by the Scandinavian response, I felt this would be a good market to explore. So in addition to Gunner and Bjorn, I engaged agents in Denmark and Finland. I then set about undertaking a personal tour in 1977 to research all four countries while working with the agents and meeting buyers. This was followed by regular visits until the early 80s, and I developed a worthwhile turnover, coupled with some humorous memories.

Finland is a country of lakes, with as much water as land, close to Russia, with a language impossible to comprehend. After the first day's work in Helsinki, I was invited to dinner at my agent's home in a village some ten miles from the city. During the meal, I was surprised at the amount of brandy consumed, knowing the strict laws that prevailed on alcohol. When it was time to leave, my host bid me good night, showed me to the door, and to my complete bewilderment left me standing in the street. I wandered around for ages trying to thumb a lift and eventually managed to stop a taxi, which took me back to my hotel. The following morning I confronted my agent who retorted, "Surely you didn't expect me to drive in such a condition?" Strange, but a lesson learned.

Norway, of course, is a beautiful, breathtaking country, and although we established business in Bergen, Algard, Drammen, and Trondheim, Oslo was the centre of commercial activity. Gunner Birkevold came from a wealthy family in Aalesund in the north and commuted to the capital, making his base at the famous deluxe Grand Hotel where a suite was always reserved in his name. He never wore a watch, but if you asked him the time he would hum for a moment then give you the precise time. Like most Norwegians, he was solidly built and well over six feet tall with a weird sense of humour, but his connections led to many substantial orders. I was generally away from home two to three weeks at a time in order to cover four countries over widespread areas and one weekend I was unable to leave my hotel in Bergen due to torrential rain. Accepting the situation, and with the aid of countless flasks of coffee, I spent long hours revising for my senior athletics coach exam. On another occasion I enjoyed a fascinating two days with Gunner and his wife touring the fjords on a small boat with sleeping accommodations.

Since my previous visit to Denmark, I had appointed different agents, the latest being Axsel Jensen, who proved to be well known and well connected. However Karl, the one I engaged in 1977, did not last long. He had a remarkable history: during the war, for a fee, he enjoyed no fewer than sixteen honeymoons by marrying women then smuggling them across the North Sea to safety in Britain. It must have had some effect on his personality: when walking down the street to our first appointment in Copenhagen, he suddenly passed the sample bag to me, clutched his crotch, exclaiming, "Oh my onions!" and promptly disappeared. Luckily I had a list of calls and made my way to the intended destination, hoping he would arrive there. This he did, an hour later, and on our way through the store he stopped at the lingerie counter where he purchased a pair of flimsy briefs, then made a present of them to the girl who served him. *Hell,* I thought, *what have I done?* Later I discovered that his absence from the street was to liaise with a nurse living nearby who had the same sexual tendencies as himself.

We got through the week with some success. On the Friday before leaving, I was looking to buy Doris a homecoming present and was attracted by a nice leather manicure set. While in the shop Karl kept eying the sales girl and before leaving said, "My friend here is departing for home tomorrow and is having a farewell party tonight and would like you to come." The surprised girl replied, "But sir, I am a married woman." "Good references," Karl replied. Needless to say, I had to change the agency.

Once we became established, several Danish customers visited us at our showroom. While in Manchester, we wined and dined them in style. One prominent buyer promised to reciprocate when I was next in Copenhagen. He did so by treating me to a hamburger and coffee from a cardboard cup outside in a stall in the main square saying, "I thought you would like something different." The Danes have a reputation for being known as the 'Scrooges of Scandinavia' and I was warned that I should count my fingers after shaking hands!

Sweden is a massive country and hundreds of miles separated each call. It was not unusual to have to dig the car out of snow in the mornings, and spiked wheels were compulsory in the Winter time. One day we were late for an appointment, and I was aghast when Bjorn drove his car down the slope of a lake, then crossed the ice to the other side. Travel was always hazardous, and once I watched the small plane in which we were travelling being de-iced literally just before take off. I always started at Bjorn's home in Gothenburg, then travelled the long distances to such places as Stockholm, Boras, and Malmo on endless roads through pine forests. We opened many of the top accounts, and on one visit to Almhult, in central Sweden, we turned down a small order from the now universally famous IKEA, which had only been offered on condition that they would have world exclusive copyright on the selected design.

Bjorn Sjoberg believed he was God's gift to women and took pains to explain that life in Sweden was completely different to the UK. For example, he and his wife would go out on separate nights, then exchange their experiences afterwards. He was a tall, very blond, good looking character and, like George Holland and Malcolm Allison, had a certain magnetism for the opposite sex. Wherever we travelled in Sweden, he was always on the lookout for a big band night, very popular at certain top hotels, where he could exercise his charms. One night, we were staying at the Grand Hotel in Boras after the local team had heavily defeated a Scottish club that afternoon and put them out of the European Cup. The bar and dance area was full of joyous Swedes and desperate Scots, but one particular person really got on my nerves. He was a rival agent to Bjorn and moved around humiliating and ridiculing the Scots and I felt he should be taught a lesson. I asked Bjorn if he spoke English then invited him to join us at our table.

When Mr Big Mouth was seated, I explained that I had the authority to represent Manchester United and was empowered to bestow a prestigious honour provided he could answer three questions. He was instantly interested and my first question was, did he know the name of the ground where Manchester United played? "Old Trafford," he replied, and I duly nodded. Second, did he know the name of the Manchester United manager, correctly answering Matt Busby. I then went on to the third question asking him to name the famous player whose first name was Bobby and he replied, "Charlton," of course. "Well done," I said, "I can now award you the title of a Manchester United Prick," and I suggested that he should announce this honour from the stage. So when the music stopped, with the consent of the band leader, Mr Big Mouth proudly and loudly told everybody that he was now a 'Manchester United Prick' much to the delight of my Scottish friends who fell about laughing and bombarded me with drinks for most of the evening. Bjorn and I worked well together and became well known throughout Sweden as 'The Terrible Twins' and got the most out of the market until a considerable change of styles.

Doris and I proudly attended the graduation of both our children at Birmingham University in July 1979, when coincidentally they were both honoured in the same week. Lisa received her Medical degree and Stephen was awarded a 2.1 in Business Studies & Economics. It was an emotional experience for us remembering our humble beginnings, and it gave us grateful satisfaction.

I kept in touch with Manchester City, who had won the League Cup in 1976 and were runners up in the First Division in the 1976/77 season, Liverpool pipping us by one point. In 1979 there was an unnecessary mass clear out, and with the retirement of Colin Bell, the club took a downward turn.

14

My annual trips to the West Indies continued, but with Jamaica out of the equation and Nassau turning to America, I was looking for replacement trade. Barbados was static and I wondered how I could increase turnover. Over a drink one night I heard there was a good business to be had with the coloured population and discussed this with Tony Lawless. He reluctantly agreed and stated that Geddes Grant had not encouraged this due to colonial tradition. However, if I was interested he could put me in touch with an Indian member of his staff who might have the necessary connections.

She duly visited me at my hotel and said she could organise a meeting with a group of peddlers, but this could only be arranged at certain times due to religious commitments. Consequently she fixed a date between prayer meetings of 6.00 p.m. at a nearby house and together we waited on a large flat roof with my samples. Just before the appointed time, a number of vans drove up, and at least a dozen bearded Indians in white robes greeted us in their customary manner. Their leader addressed me in an educated Oxford accent through his thick, black, beard, informing me that he was the head of the group who earned their living selling from carts in the country districts. If I displayed my samples, he would invite individual requirements that would be accumulated into a bulk order and the goods duly distributed to each party on arrival of each shipment. I had practised this kind of system in South Africa and with my customers all seated, cross legged around me in a circle, I did my stuff with my friend from Geddes Grant taking notes. Promptly at 7.00 p.m. the group disbanded and departed for the mosque, with the usual two handed bowed gesture from each individual in turn, and in one hour I had taken the largest furnishing fabric order in the company's Bajan history. Payment was prompt, but when a number of the group later visited the Geddes Grant showrooms, they had to enter through the rear door.

Looking further afield I learned that the Dutch West Indies (Netherlands Antilles) was open to imports. Aruba, Bonaire, and Curacao, known as the ABC islands, appeared to have its business centre in Willemstad, the capital of Curacao. With the help of the Manchester Chamber of Commerce, I located an agent called M.P. Jacobina, generally known by his surname. He provisionally agreed to represent me, and was there to meet me from my Trinidad flight in February 1980. Jacobina was a small, strong, wiry native of Curacao, in his late sixties without a grey hair on his head and had thirty-four grandchildren. It soon became apparent that he was well known and respected, and I made a good choice in confirming his agency appointment. We did the rounds in Curacao and the nearby island of Aruba and were successful in taking initial orders with most of the best accounts.

The next year I allowed more time and the day after my arrival Jacobina collected me from my hotel on my fifty-first birthday. I had enjoyed a successful trip in Barbados and Trinidad, was fit and bronzed, and feeling like a twenty-one year old asked Jacobina how old he thought I was. He drove along in silence for a while then to my horror and disbelief he said, "Seventy." My whole world fell apart and when I questioned why, he replied, "Because you have snow on top." I had always been prematurely grey and now felt somewhat better.

We got more and more into the market in 1982, and while in Aruba, I could not understand why I could sell about 20,000 metres annually to a population of only 10,000. Jacobina said to meet him at midnight and I would have my answer. We drove to the tip of the island, just across the water from Venezuela. There, to my amazement, I witnessed my goods being loaded into rowing boats for sale in Caracas where duty on furnishings was extortionate. An arrangement was made for the customs officers to turn their backs when the boats arrived on the other side and vans transported rolls of fabrics to local markets.

On another trip, I was having coffee with a member of the Sabga family at his office in Port of Spain. His office was on the first floor and built with a large, wide, glass partition overlooking the store so he could observe everything that was going on below. Every now and again he glanced with annoyance at a small bearded man who kept waving up at him. Losing patience, he sent his secretary down to have him removed, but when she returned it transpired that the stranger knew him, and he was brought up to the office. "Don't you know me?" the man said, "I used to room at your house when studying at Trinidad University." "Of course, forgive me," Sabga replied giving him a hug, saying, "I didn't recognise you with your beard, what are you doing now?" "I am the prime minister of Curacao," he answered, "and being in town on a political mission thought I would look you up."

After the embarrassing start, I joined in the conversation for the rest of the morning and explained that I would be leaving for Curacao the following day. Upon departing, he gave me his card and his direct telephone number and asked me to contact him if he could be of service during my stay.

On previous visits, I had always made my base in Willemstad, but looking for a change had decided on the only beach hotel in Curacao. After checking in I was shown to a small dark room and could not believe how bad it was. There were no windows, the temperature was stifling and there was no way I could sleep there. Returning to reception, I complained to the manager and was told that was it. I then turned to his secretary and asked her to get me the prime minister on the phone, giving her the direct number. After acknowledging he was on the line, she nervously handed the phone over to me with the whole of the hotel staff gathered around. "Hello my friend, how are you?" said the prime minister, "I didn't think I would be hearing from you so soon, where are you staying?" I looked at the manager and told him that the prime minister had asked me where I was staying and was I being looked after. "Tell him yes," the red faced manager stuttered, and after a few courteous words with the prime minister, I hung up.

An American couple occupying the best suite in the hotel were moved on to accommodate me, and thereafter I was treated like a lord during my few days stay. Upon leaving, I requested my bill, refusing to accept charity, and the head receptionist said, "I know you, you are Howard Hughes, known to be friends with kings and prime ministers." I just smiled and said goodbye.

Aruba was at one time a virtual desert island, made rich by the installation of an oil refinery that brought mass employment and prosperity. The capital is Oranjestad, with the other commercial area being Saint Nicolas. In 1984, Jacobina arranged a one-day trip with appointments in both territories. After arriving early morning, we had completed our programme in Oranjestad, but siesta time meant we could not find a taxi to take us to Saint Nicolas. Time was limited, so we decided to walk. The area between the two towns was desolate, with just one adjoining road. As we made our way, a police van suddenly pulled up in front of us, and we were unceremoniously bungled, without explanation, into the back by two large, uniformed gorilla types. Upon arriving at a police station, we were manhandled into the hallway to be greeted by an even more ferocious sergeant who accused us of being drug merchants as otherwise why would we be walking with a case at that time of day in such heat.

"Look in the case," I said, "and you will see that there are only textile samples." but he refused to do so.

Jacobina was getting more and more agitated and strenuously objected to their attitude, saying they were completely out of order and insulting to me, a guest of the country. "Shut up little man," the sergeant reacted and pushed Jacobina to the floor. I saw red and attacked the big thug and within seconds found myself being held down with a gun to my head. With my arms twisted up my back, I was then thrown into jail and was told to sit on a high stool, with a gun still at my head, and informed in no uncertain terms that I would be shot if I moved. The jail was filthy, with no air, and the stench from the other prisoners was sickening. I remained that way for what seemed like an eternity. After about two hours the jail door was opened and I was pushed back into the hallway to be received by two gentlemen in white suits, one of which was the British Consulate whom Jacobina had contacted. I was advised not to utter a single word and told I would be set free provided

I consented to a deportation order to be out of Aruba by midnight. Although I was very angry, I held my tongue, and we were dropped off in Saint Nicolas, being reminded of the deportation condition, which meant prison if I failed to comply.

Meanwhile Jacobina had telephoned the buyers to explain what had happened and they all agreed to see me early in the evening, and with apologies for the way I had been treated, placed good sympathy orders.

Upon contacting the airport we found there were no scheduled flights back to Curacao and we had to hire a private plane to get us back in time to meet the deadline. I was horrified when we boarded the small aircraft whose wings seemed to have been stuck on with chewing gum. As luck would have it, we encountered a severe tropical storm just after take-off and were flung about a black, oily sky lit up by fork lightening, accompanied by deafening peals of thunder. For the second time in the day I felt my number was up, but we eventually landed safely in Curacao in the early hours. Jacobina then insisted that we call on a friend of his on our way from the airport who was the editor of the local newspaper and the story appeared the following day. The editor explained that I was a very lucky man, because an American had been shot dead the previous week in a similar incident. Aruba was a police state at the time, so there was nothing that could be done.

Apart from one final visit in 1985 this was to be the end of trade with the Netherlands Antilles as the refinery closure in Aruba resulted in total redundancy. The island and its beautiful silver sand beaches were later converted into a holiday resort for the rich, with the mafia moving in to build luxury hotels and casinos.

A similar situation with the oil refineries took place in San Fernando in Trinidad. With the shortage of money, and the introduction of enforced import restrictions, my visits and adventures in the West Indies ended.

However, the family's association with Barbados did not end. In 1978, as part of her medical degree, Lisa spent two months on the island studying eye disease and resided at the Queen Elizabeth hospital. Tony Lawless took her under his wing and introduced her into the local Bajan society, making her stay both pleasant and memorable. Their friendship has been ongoing over the years, and Lisa later spent several holidays in Barbados.

Lisa returned to the area as a qualified doctor and was married in August 1980. Two years later, in August 1982, Stephen married Lynne, whom he had known since he was seventeen, and they also made their home in Sale. Our first grandchild, Gareth, was born to Lisa in 1983, followed by Laura in 1985 and Rhiannon in 1988. Stephen became the proud father of Lauren in 1987 and Jordan in 1992, and it was a blessing for Doris and I to have five fine and healthy grandchildren.

15

The textile trade in the UK had taken a dramatic turn, and the wholesale business was almost nonexistent. Large retail groups now monopolised the home market, and even independent stores had the clout to buy direct. As we had specialised on piece goods (priced by the yard) and in the less popular woven brocades, our turnover had diminished considerably. The situation was worsened by the loss of overseas orders.

The company reached a crisis point, so we had to move with the times or go. A drastic policy change was called for, but my sales and production management staff were nearing retirement age and did not seem to have the energy, invention, or desire to meet the challenge. Also the modern British housewife had no time or patience to sew and make up curtains anymore, and the future appeared to be ready-made curtains. These were already being produced by competitors who were offering designs and colours, mainly in prints, in a variety of sizes which were simply taken from a pack and hung at a window. This was an obvious avenue to explore, with different skills in manufacture and presentation required, but the innovation was not foreign to me, because I had experimented with the theory in the mid-seventies.

The company had to be reinvented with new, young ideas, and a different outlook was required. After one sales appointment disaster, I placed a local advertisement and my son Stephen applied for an interview. His first job had been financial reporting with an engineering company in Horwich. At the time he was working for Ron Hill Sports in a marketing capacity. He insisted that if he was to be considered for the position I must ignore the fact that he was my son. He joined the company in February 1982 on merit, spending the early part of his new career studying textile manufacture. Between us, in an effort to diversify, we tried mail order and sports kit promotion, but without any measured success, so we decided to concentrate on the development of ready-made curtains, where Stephen could use his creative skills.

I was then faced with the problem of reorganisation, and my sales director and general manager accepted early retirement on full pay up to their sixty-fifth birthdays. As the company was desperately short of cash this had to come out of my savings, but I was happy to make the gesture as both had been loyal and conscientious, always giving their best.

The problem now was to introduce different products and build a new customer base with little money in the pot to expand. A good deal of investigation and research was necessary, and once again I had to go out on the road for weeks on end, economising whenever I could by travelling third class and staying at low-cost hotels. One time, escaping from my £10 per night accommodation in Pimlico (which I had to pay in advance), I walked the streets of London from 7 p.m. to 3 a.m. the following morning allowing my thoughts to wander. I passed the Houses of Parliament several times and at the end of my journey had decided that instead of continuing with the traditional sales director/ sales manager approach, major transactions would be conducted from the top to the top. This would constitute a key house account plan where negotiations and discussions to acquire bulk orders would be at the highest level, reflecting an image of greater importance when seeking appointments and leading to vital direct marketing information. The rest of the UK would be served by agents payable on commission, and although the nucleus of these were already with the company, gaps had to be filled to cover the whole of the country.

Once this had been established I accompanied each agent personally to give them confidence and belief in the company's future, which was essential in order to have their full support. In every region, the best top accounts were chosen and designs confined exclusively, thereby giving the customer an advantage over competitors.

On the supply side, contacts were made with two print works. We created our own designs from paintings, then sought out privately-owned factories to manufacture the curtains. Through the generations, my family has been artistically gifted, and Stephen was no exception, having obtained an A level in art. His understanding of design and colour was an important factor in the selection and development of ideas. Also, he installed computer systems, which greatly improved efficiencies in all sections of the company.

The overall strategy proved to be successful, and little by little, throughout the 80s and well into the 90s, 'Homemaker' ready-made curtains became an admired and well respected brand.

Sport has always been a significant part of my life. Aside from the pure love of it, it has served to be a distraction from pressures and stress. For the next two decades and more my sporting life was mostly committed to athletics, described separately in *Life in Athletics,* but I had not forgotten my football roots. Manchester City has always been high on my agenda, and in 1993 Francis Lee took over an ailing club, giving the fans and myself fresh hope. He formed a new Board of Directors and quickly enforced structural changes. For example, after I returned to Maine Road, the same large crack, there since my playing days in the 50s, was still evident in the home dressing room bath. The changing facilities for the players were quickly resolved, and the grey concrete interior of the home stand was replaced by suites, restaurants, and bars. The administration staff made room by moving to a nearby Victorian house in Fallowfield.

Francis raised much needed capital by offering tables in the Board Room Suite restaurant to companies for a loan of £50,000 each. He built an extra level in the Kippax Stand to accommodate additional corporate seating and a large dining area with magnificent views over the city. He also instituted the now famous Youth Academy at Platt Lane, which would bring a flow of talented youngsters through the ranks. More investment was still needed, and in late 1994, I met Mike Summerbee for the first time over a cup of coffee at Maine Road and agreed to purchase fifty thousand shares in the club, which I added to over the next four years.

My association with City was rejuvenated, and after meeting Francis, I became acquainted with former players such as Tony Book , Dennis Tueart, and Johnnie Williamson, together with Bernard Halford, Geoff

Durbin, Alex Williams, and many others from behind the scenes. I got to know Colin Bell under different circumstances as his son, Jon, competed in the high jump for Sale Harriers, and his daughter, Dawn, was no mean sprinter. Acquaintances were also renewed with Dave Ewing and Ken Barnes, and later I had a laugh with Bert Trautmann on his cure for my football boots, and Roy and Kath Clark became friends of Doris and myself.

To secure additional funds Francis Lee organised open-air concerts at Maine Road, and on a warm, magical night in June, with Geoff Durbin and his wife, Doris and I watched Rod Stewart at his best, following Bon Jovi's opening act, from the Director's Box overlooking the pitch. A high, circular stage had been centrally erected, and with an orchestra playing underneath, Rod Stewart and his band's performance was spectacular. As part of his show, while still singing, Rod bounded about the stage and juggled and kicked footballs into the adoring crowd surrounding the stage. Having been invited for a meal after the concert we sat within touching distance of the top table where Rod Stewart joined Francis Lee, Mike Summerbee, Denis Law, George Best, Malcolm Allison, and Alan Ball. Being mad about football, Rod was in his element, always flying to watch Scotland whenever he could, wherever he was touring in the world and has his own full size pitch at his South England home.

I sat in the executive box on match days with Doris and members of my family and enjoyed the banter before and after the games in the international lounge, where Tudor Thomas had his very special museum. A character who will always stay in my memory is Neil Midgley, one of the best referees ever, who died prematurely in 2001. His warm personality and unique sense of humour can never be forgotten. He presided over the monthly sportsmen's luncheons held in the Board Room Suite, hosted by Mike Summerbee, who invited me to join the top table. This gave me an opportunity to share the day with some of soccer's greats. Amongst others, I got to meet Nat Lofthouse, Billy Bremner, Peter Osgood, Emlyn Hughes, Tommy Docherty, Norman Hunter, and Tommy Smith, and I found their company absorbing. Personalities such as Freddie Truman from cricket, John Willie McBride of rugby fame, boxing champions, politicians, and stars from show business also made appearances, and it was a privilege spending time with them. Mike knew them all and they all knew Mike.

Although I had the honour of meeting Sir Tom Finney, I have always regretted not having shaken hands with Stanley Matthews. He and Peter Doherty, were my boyhood heroes. On three occasions, I was due to meet Stanley through a friend of mine in Stoke, but each time I was prevented from doing so. Stanley played in the First Division at the age of fifty and, incredibly, took part in a match in Africa when he was eighty. He combined his genius with unbelievable hard work and dedication and was deservedly knighted, if only for the example he set to others.

After the disastrous choice of Alan Ball as manager, City were relegated from the Premiership in 1996, and in 1998 Francis resigned after four years of dedication and strife, although it has never been publicly disclosed just how much he did for the club. David Bernstein, whom Francis had appointed as his financial director, took over as chairman and Joe Royle was brought in as manager, with Willy Donachie as his head coach and assistant. I had great respect for Willy with his supreme fitness and man management methods. He lived close by and knew of my coaching background. Early in July, just before the new season, Joe, Willy, and Asa Hartford brought the whole of the first team squad to Wythenshawe Park where I had arranged for them to use the running track for fitness assessment. Each player was monitored after clocking 3000 metres.

Thereafter they engaged in endurance work for a week or so, then returned to the track for further analysis before beginning a programme of technical work. This project was repeated preseason in 1999. In June 2000, Willy asked if I would meet him in the Platt Lane complex to address a group of players who required extra preseason preparation. I duly obliged, and after Willy had introduced me as a coach with both football and athletic knowledge, I agreed to knock them into shape. Terry Cooke, Tony Grant, Lee Crook, Robert Taylor, and Lee Peacock were in the group and I compiled conditioning schedules that included sessions of working together twice a week out in the country. These consisted of steady runs, circuits of alternative jogging and sprinting round a football pitch, hill running, and occasionally continuous relays. I recruited Gareth, my grandson, who was at the time training with the Harriers, to run with and pace the group, and being a true blue he enjoyed working with the players. I was also able to help with suggestions on diet and personal advice and regularly reported back to both Joe and Willy on progress, or lack of it.

Unfortunately, Joe left City under a cloud in 2001, taking Willy with him. Joe was and still is full of wit and humour and described City's historical and breathtaking win against Gillingham at Wembley in 1989 as a 'rocking chair moment', when the fans who witnessed the pulsating ending would still remember the day when they are old in their rocking chairs.

City has always been a family club, ever generous to a cause or a personal need. Jean Kehoe, who helped me at Sale Harriers, told me of her elderly father, a lifelong City fan, who could recite any team in full and any match score going back the 1930s. His one remaining ambition was to see City play again, and after I had mentioned this to the management, they said they would do all possible to make him welcome. Jean drove to Blackpool where he lived, and I collected them both from her home in Sale to take them to Maine Road. I was absolutely flabbergasted by his accurate knowledge and history of the club and just by mentioning the year he rattled out the team, scores and sometimes even the attendance. We seated him in the reception area for a while, and Georgi Kinkladze and some of the other players made a fuss of him. Unfortunately, the game did not live up to expectation, being a 0–0 draw with Stockport County, but much to his surprise and delight he was introduced over the public address system at half time. After the game I drove him back to Jean's, but sadly soon after his return to Blackpool he took ill, never recovered, and fell into a coma. I only learned of this when I delivered a City programme to Jean that contained her father's photograph. Jean took this to Blackpool for him and later told me that although her father did not appear to be conscious at the time, she talked to him about the photograph. Somehow he seemed to know and squeezed her hand just before dying.

16

Early in 1997 Trevor Baxter, a sportswriter for the *Manchester Evening News,* telephoned me to see if I would like to attend the annual Sports Personality of the Year awards luncheon at the Midland Hotel, Manchester in late January. I replied that as this would conflict with a very busy time for me it would be doubtful that I could make it, but would let him know. Several more phone calls followed and I could not understand his persistence. As it happened, the buyer who was due to call at my office that day cancelled at the last minute, and I was able to tell Trevor that I could be there. I then hurriedly asked my close friend and assistant athletic manager, Bill Nicholls, if he would like a free lunch, and he donned his smart blazer to accompany me.

On arrival, and after checking in at the reception desk, a large cross was placed by my name, but at the time I did not think anything of this. Not really knowing just what to expect I was amazed at the magnitude of the occasion where 350 plus guests were gathered in a huge dining hall, complete with a large stage and giant screen. I was further surprised when we were shown to a front table, close to the stage, next to David Beckham and other well known sports personalities. "Why are we here?" I said to Bill and he replied, "It's better than being at the back." Des Lynam was the Master of Ceremonies and the place started to buzz as music was played and Alistair McGowan gave hilarious impressions of people in sport.

After lunch came the awards with champion boxer Robbie Reid winning the 1996 Sports Personality of the year and Bobbie Goulding from St Helens Rugby League runner-up. David Beckham was next on stage as the 1996 Young Sports Personality of the Year, with just the Sir Matt Busby Lifetime Achievement Award left to conclude the programme. Previous recipients had been Sir Clive Lloyd and Sir Bobby Charlton, and I glanced around at the famous faces wondering who was going to win this year. Des Lynam explained the significance of the award and began to provide background on the would-be winner, and in a daze I realised, "My God, he's talking about me."

After the introduction I was invited on to the stage. Pat Crerand made the presentation in place of Matt's son Sandy, who was prevented from being there. One journalist described me as a 'stunned Eric Hughes', and this was putting it mildly. Des then interviewed me (I was aware of the huge image of myself on the screen) and asked me about my life in sport. In my thank you response, I mumbled that it was an even greater honour as all the previous winners had all held knighthoods. "Never mind," Des said, "How does Sir Eric sound?" I am still waiting. It was an even greater privilege to be officially associated with Sir Matt, whom I had known and respected so much.

Still in shock, I spent the next hour talking to TV and radio presenters and newspaper reporters, then clutching my cut glass trophy made my way home to share the moment with Doris. The following year, Alex Ferguson received the Sir Matt Busby award, and I wrote congratulating him, saying that we were the only two 'commoners' to have the honour, adding this would be short-lived in his case. Sure enough I wrote to him the next year to congratulate him on his knighthood.

It was also a very important year for my wife Doris. When she had been evacuated to a Staffordshire village during the war, she struck up a friendship with an American pen-pal, which has lasted for more than half a century. In 1942, a school in Illinois sent gift parcels for British evacuees in Cheddleton where Doris was living, and she wrote a letter of thanks to America that was published in a local newspaper. Leora Fatland read this, and from a farm in her home town of Joliet wrote to Doris, 3000 miles away, sowing the seeds for a wonderful lasting friendship.

Both girls were of a similar age and with words have shared their experiences of life through primary school, secondary school, getting engaged, being married, having children, then grandchildren. Yet they did not meet until June 1997 when Leora (now Compton) toured

Europe with husband Dan as members of a choir, also performing in St Petersburg, Russia, and extended their trip to visit the UK. And so after 55 years of writing to each other regularly, they met at last, both wondering how it would be. Leora and Dan flew to London, then hired a car to bring them North for a rendezvous in the unspectacular setting of the Knutsford service station car park. Nervously waiting, the moment finally arrived and the girls affectionately embraced. Leora later said that it was everything they imagined it would be. Doris added that it was as if they had always known each other. There could never be such a warm and happy relationship which started so long ago and is still as strong today.

Kevin Keegan was installed as City's manager in 2001, promptly signed Stewart Pearce as his captain, and won the First Division Championship by a canter in his first season, collecting more than one hundred league goals. The fans were delighted to witness free flowing, attacking football, and City came in ninth in the Premiership the following year. Kevin, with his infectious personality, vastly improved the image of the Club and the training facilities at Carrington, recruiting skilled coaches to work with a squad that now included top names attracted by his worldwide reputation.

The new fitness coach was Juan Carlos Osario, brought in from Colombia via the States, whose methods were totally different to that of Willy Donachie. Instead of long endurance runs, training was over short, repetitive distances with more ball skills. This excluded my brief football coaching role, but I was invited to Carrington to work with Juan Carlos who was highly qualified and possessed two master's degrees. I was so exhausted after the day's varied sessions afterwards that I had to soak in a hot bath for ages to relieve my aches and pains. His concepts were brilliant and inventive, and he was interested in what I could offer in speed development from athletics. I joined Kevin, the coaches, and players for lunch and on the whole enjoyed the experience.

I discovered that Kevin was superstitious like myself, and we shared lucky number seven. Everything I do in life is influenced by seven, or in multiples of seven, for example I complete all my exercises in series of seven and when I fill up with petrol seven must appear either in litres or on the cash receipt. When City beat United, 3-1, in the last derby match at Maine Road in November 2002, the kick-off time was 12.07 hours and the second half began at 13.07 hours, enough said.

After a disappointing 2004–2005 season, Kevin Keegan left, but he will always be fondly remembered for his charisma, hard work, enthusiasm, and the contribution he made to the progression of the Club. Who could not like the man whom I admired for his knowledge, quick mind, intelligence, and the confidence he inspired in players.

Meanwhile, in 2002 the most important sporting event in the history of Manchester was about to take place—the XVII Commonwealth Games.

Some ten years earlier, as part of its generation process, Manchester City Council had envisioned building a stadium in East Manchester. When they were awarded the Commonwealth Games, this became a reality. The Council obtained funding from central government, Sports England, and the Lottery, conditional on an anchor tenant being guaranteed once the Games were over. There could be no risk of a £110 million white elephant standing unoccupied; fortunately the problem was solved when Manchester City FC agreed to take over the stadium.

The two Bernsteins, Sir Howard, the Chief Executive of the Council, and David, the Chairman of City, got their heads together, and with meticulous planning ensured there would be first class athletic facilities for the Games and a state of the art football stadium afterwards. As the size of an athletic track is different to a football pitch, three permanent stands were initially built with a temporary stand on the north side. This would be replaced by a permanent matching stand after the Games to perfect the final shape of the stadium, which was christened the City of Manchester Stadium. The athletic field was initially constructed twenty feet higher than the proposed football pitch and millions of tons of soil buried the first few rows in the lower tiers. This was later removed, the soil being employed in banking and landscaping the nearby warm up area which would, in due course, be converted into a smaller athletic stadium.

Work began immediately after the conclusion of the most successful Commonwealth Games ever, the track was torn up and digging took place down to the required level, unveiling space for an extra 10,000 seats. The north stand was erected without delay and by working night and day completion of the internal structure was ready for the 2002–2003 football season.

However, there was an outcry from certain quarters that the track should remain untouched and the stadium retained as the country's national athletic centre. A number of well-known international athletes endorsed this, claiming they had never performed in a better arena with such a great atmosphere. Having been involved with both sports from the outset, I publicly defended the change over and reiterated that if Manchester City FC had not agreed to move across town, the stadium would not have been there for Paula Radcliffe, Jonathan Edwards, Ashia Hansen, and others to win their gold medals. Also, although the Games had been a sell-out, this would not have been the case for a normal athletic meeting, and I indicated that plans were under way for alternative options.

Although I was excited at the prospect of City playing in such a magnificent new stadium, I felt very sad to be leaving Maine Road. Memories flooded back from sneaking into the ground at three-quarter time as a schoolboy, to training in the fifties, and watching some unforgettable matches. On 15 May 2003, Mike Summerbee and David Chell organised a nostalgic 'end-of-an-era' luncheon in the suite on top of the Kippax Street stand, and there were some misty eyes looking down on the pitch remembering days gone by.

Once the Games were over and City had taken over the stadium, the nearby athletic warm-up area was transformed into a 6000-seat outdoor stadium with a linked indoor arena, both ideal for holding competitions of the highest standard (more details appear in *Life in Athletics*). Together with provision for a variety of other sports, these facilities enhanced the unique and impressive complex now famously known as Sportcity, which undoubtedly equals, or possibly betters, anything the rest of Europe has to offer.

The textile trade had once more changed drastically; UK production had ceased to exist, and importation from such countries as China and Pakistan had taken over. This meant adopting new techniques by developing our ideas in Manchester and having them made thousands of miles away in our own packaging.

My life continued to be full, retaining a business interest, having increased responsibilities in athletics and ongoing football commitments. Doris rarely missed a City home match, and I joined Mike Summerbee and Fred Ayre at regular sportsmen's luncheons with other blue friends and former players.

In the early days, when Doris and I first married, without a penny in the world, our hope was to try to create a family dynasty to give our children and grandchildren a better start to life. Lisa had risen as a consultant to a high position in medical circles, and Stephen now ran the company to meet new challenges. Our grandchildren did us proud: Gareth graduated from Oxford in 2004 winning a Blue, captaining the cross country team. Laura followed her mother's footsteps by achieving a medical degree in 2008 at Nottingham University. Rhiannon and Lauren were both studying at Leeds University in 2006, and the youngest, Jordan, was showing great creative promise at Sale Grammar.

One day I stood on the forecourt of Sportcity with the City stadium on my right and the athletics stadium on my left, reflecting on the moments in my life. The skinny kid from the slums of Salford, the two teenagers with little means who had grown a dynasty, the hazards of business and highlights of sport. Above all I thanked God for having Doris by my side and giving our family such good health and success.

Perhaps 'little by little' I had got there.

Life in Athletics

1

I hung up my football boots in 1964, and like so many in the sport, turned to golf. I joined Sale Golf Club to be instructed by the local professional. Somehow, I could not adopt the recognised basics and in particular felt awkward addressing the ball on the tee. Also I had the distinct urge to take off after the ball down the fairway and began to think golf was not for me. I nearly gave up, but a friend advised, "You are a natural ball player, play like one." Being duly inspired, I quickly got my handicap down from twenty-four to sixteen, but realised that with a young family and business responsibilities, I could never achieve single figures. That required continuous and dedicated practice. Although it was fun playing with Malcolm Allison, Noel Cantwell, and other sportsmen, I found it difficult to hang around in competitions against slow-scoring opponents who felt it was appropriate to buy champagne if they broke one hundred. I missed track suit sport. I did not believe that even if I was successful at golf that it would give me adequate fulfilment.

My life in athletics began in September 1969 when Lisa (13 years) decided she enjoyed running and would like to join Sale Harriers who trained at Crossford Bridge, Sale. Like many other interested parents, my wife and I supported Lisa, following her progress and taking her to races and competitions, which mostly constituted cross country and road running. Stephen (11 years) joined the Harriers in Spring 1970 and quickly won his place in the Colts team.

Later in August, on a family holiday in Abersoch, the senior Sale middle-distance coach, Alan Robertshaw, was staying nearby and personally supervised endurance sessions for Lisa and Stephen. He put them through such training as sand hill running and water treading, and later we all played soccer on the beach. Alan already had knowledge of my coaching background and worked on me over the two weeks, persuading me to become involved at Sale. I agreed to learn all I could about athletics with a view to possibly taking an active part in management and was elected to the Committee in October 1970, promising to make Sale Harriers a dominant national force.

Joe Lancaster, a former world record holder and journalist, interviewed me and published a prominent article in the *Times* outlining my thoughts on the 'ancient sport of athletics', stating that this was run by 'tin gods' who were more interested in their own power than the sport itself, which could not be improved unless drastic changes were made.

The hierarchy took note and exception to this and waited for an opportunity to throw me out of athletics.

Their opportunity came at the Frodsham Hill races in September 1970, when I inadvertently gave a wrong number to an athlete, Kelvin Breeze. Although basically I was without fault, I was summoned with the team, to appear in Liverpool on 8 January 1971 before the entire Northern Counties Committee. I was interrogated for forty-five minutes by fourteen members of the Committee. The hearing started at 8.00 p.m., and I waited until 10.40 p.m. for the verdict. Incredibly, I was banned for a period of six months, not even being allowed to go near any athlete or athletic facility. This took my breath away, and I accused the meeting of unfair and unacceptable action, stating that 'the kid gloves were now off' and promised that such injustice would not be tolerated. This was treated with apparent scorn, but, after taking the name and address of every person present, on 20 January 1971, I gave notice of appeal supported by legal proceedings.

Again the story made the news, and I swore I would see justice done whatever the cost in time or expenditure, not just for my sake, but for the sake of others.

Joe Lancaster introduced me to Jack Davies, a senior partner with a well-known Manchester solicitor who had expert knowledge of athletics.

He, in turn, suggested I should approach Mr John Hugnill, Barrister, who had recently made national headlines on winning the George Eastham case, which gave professional footballers the right to choose the club they could play for when transferred. Although now a famous name, John Hugnill agreed to represent me, being a firm believer in justice and fair play.

Meanwhile, I was prevented from even watching athletics, which included the possibility of the Under 15s Sale girls winning a first ever national Cross Country title. I was not going to miss the race under any circumstances and hid in the back of Alan Robertshaw's van to the course then sheltered behind trees to shout the girls on to the gold medals.

By coincidence, at the same time, Malcolm Allison of Manchester City was banned from football, and we spent some of the leisure time now available to us kicking a ball about on a nearby playing field with our children.

After much debate, the authorities decided to hold a Court of Appeal by the AAA on 2 April 1971 at the Windsor Hotel, London, chaired by Harold Abrahams, famed by the film *Chariots of Fire*.

This was a lengthy affair; the whole of the Northern Counties Committee were ordered to attend accompanied by their legal advisors. The AAA were also fully represented and with the trio of John Hugnill, Jack Davies, and myself, there was considerable presence.

The appeal result went completely in my favour. The Northern Counties Committee were duly censored, and for the first time in history, I won costs from the AAA.

One of the most memorable moments in my life occurred in the gents toilet before the final verdict, when I found myself standing side by side with Harold Abrahams. As the film described, Mr Abrahams was victimised during his early career for his religious beliefs and the fact that he employed a professional coach when winning the 100 metres gold medal at the Paris Olympics. He rose to become one of the most respected barristers in the city and was president of the AAA at the time of the hearing. Back to the toilet, he glanced over to me and said, "Don't worry son, I know what it is like to be victimised—they won't get away with it."

For the first time in my life I almost fainted. I was outside Euston station on my way home and still remember the spot where John Hugnill and Jack Davies prevented me from toppling over—the result and relief of months of stress and pressure.

My statement after winning the appeal read:

"Every sport must be governed to uphold fair play, and with the widespread network of clubs, area and district coordination is, of course, necessary.

However, the respective Committees should stimulate, not subdue, and form a basis of encouragement to both athletes and club officials. Those involved should be fully qualified in all aspects of their responsibilities, and any person sitting in judgment on others should express himself with complete knowledge of all relevant circumstances.

Some time ago I was warned of suppression by individuals who placed greater emphasis on their own power rather than the good of athletics. If this is so they should reform or resign! This is purely an amateur sport to which a vast number of people devote many hours of their spare time and energy. These efforts should be applauded and employed constructively, not jeopardised by the 'old pals act' or a comparable situation.

I have always endorsed the opinion that athletics should be Britain's finest ambassador, and by achieving more world records, we can gain the respect of the world. This must begin at club level by a strong and inviting youth policy supported by eager and devoted coaches and officials who are looking in the same direction.

Let us work together to make athletics an even greater sport!"

There was an amazing conclusion to the case, and the following week I received over a hundred telephone calls applauding the stand I had made. Many of the callers had experienced harassment by the then tin gods and decided to follow my example by not allowing the tin gods to tread on them in future. I believe this went a long way to improving athletics at the time and eventually established a better relationship for those who compete and those who administrate. Not all those in the sport were tin gods, and there were, and still are, many wonderful people who give their time and expert skills to athletics.

2

Being a much wiser man on the background of athletics, it was now time for me to learn all I could about the technical side to complement what I believe to be management and motivation ability. I studied all I could and talked to as many people in the sport as possible to expand my knowledge.

I was now a member of a club with magnificent tradition, founded in 1892 and reformed during the early 1900s. The list of achievements was breathtaking, and the club was led by the wonderful Wilson brothers, Walter and Harold, who served as chairman and secretary.

When I first went down to the humble surroundings of Crossford Bridge I thought someone was having me on as I was introduced to Harold Wilson and Jack Frost, who was team manager at the time.

Sale were more famous as a men's and boys' middle-distance club, inspired by Alan Robertshaw and his father, Reuben, who loaded youngsters up in company vans and transported them to competitions all over the country.

I was persuaded to act as men's team manager during the 1971 track & field season and did my best to organise and coordinate team relationships. From the outset, it was obvious that even though I had run a 4 minute 10 second mile and a 2 hour 32 minute marathon, I was not accepted by the majority of the team, who associated me with soccer rather than athletics. Consequently, my ideas, based on professional sport and business organisation, were not accepted, and in frustration I withdrew from this position at the end of the season.

Even so, I had obtained first-class experience on my travels and decided that if I were to exploit my new ideas, I would have to hold the necessary credentials to support them. This included coaching at the highest possible level, so I decided initially to concentrate on sprint coaching, divorcing myself from middle-distance, in which both my children were involved.

At the time, there was only a very small membership of girls at Sale, and I offered to build a women's team from scratch provided I did it my way. This was accepted with some reluctance and the challenge was there to prove myself.

A long journey lay ahead, and although I had a good commercial background and experience in professional sport, I had to enlarge my thinking. I decided to take counsel with four of the top names in soccer whom I admired and respected.

Matt Busby advised starting, from scratch, a youth scheme to bring the athletes through from a comparatively young age. Matt was famous for his 'Busby Babes', from which he developed world-class soccer players.

Bill Shankley emphasised character and advised me to be careful whom I signed, to avoid prima donnas, and to concentrate on athletes who would work for the club. In turn, the club would work for them. Over the years, I have turned down certain top athletes on his advice and never regretted this.

Joe Mercer talked at length about team spirit, encouraging support for each other even though athletics was generally regarded as an individual sport.

Malcolm Allison gave me some great thoughts on coaching, including competitive training.

All these ideas were rolled into one, and I began by contacting local schools in South Manchester to take an interest in Sale Harriers, arranging athletic sessions at Crossford Bridge, Sale.

The middle-distance section grew very quickly, because Alan Robertshaw already had a coaching structure in place, and the Under 15s followed on their national cross country success to win titles again in 1972, 1973, 1975, 1976, 1978, and 1979. By graduating progressively, the Under 17s won in 1972, 1973, 1978, 1979, and 1980. A younger age group was introduced, and the Under 13s won in 1975 and 1977. Sale Women were now recognised as a force in middle-distance, and the seniors claimed their first titles in 1977 and 1978. This division became the backbone of the club.

Reverting to the earlier years, it was necessary to give careful attention to other disciplines such as sprinting (my speciality), hurdles, and the jumps and throws events. This was made possible from the club's existing coaching set up and recruitment from outside, including parents with an adequate background in sport who were willing to adjust to athletics.

At this time, Bill Nicholls appeared at the track with his daughter Katherine, who was interested in cross country. In Bill, I detected an exceptional person who could help build the club's future, even if he was totally different from my personality. One of the most successful partnerships ever in Women's athletics was then born, with Bill looking after the field events and myself covering track, working closely together in management. Bill attained his Senior Coach badge and additionally acquired grade one field judge status, an honour shared by his wife, Joan, who also made an invaluable contribution to the progress of the club.

Gradually we developed a team of coaches, and with the accent on youth, we began to enter Young Athletes Open Meetings, trying a number of athletes in different events. A good example of this was an established middle-distance runner who 'had a go' at high jump in a Blackpool meeting. Later in the season, she broke the Northern Counties Intermediate record.

As the youngsters were now growing up, the next stage was to join the Women's Cheshire League, which involved all age groups. Apart from middle-distance, we virtually had no seniors. It was a question of filling spaces to accumulate points. In this respect, I stood at the corner of Brooklands Road on the lookout for young women walking fast from the station and looking fit enough to eventually turn out for Sale. I then stopped and questioned them about their sporting background, with the possibility of joining the club for coaching and eventual competition. This got me in hot water with the police when I was accused of molesting, and that was the end of that, although I did succeed in recruiting several athletes.

Gradually the name of the women's team at Sale Harriers became noticed and, endorsed by local press, generated great interest. This was shown in the progress made and the growing membership in all disciplines.

On the coaching front, I had developed a good sprint group. I first came into contact with Wilf Paish, who was in charge of the Great Britain squad at the time and one of the most respected coaches in the world. Wilf became a mentor to both Bill and me, and our friendship exists to this day. He had a great impact on my coaching career, and his advice was invaluable. Coupled with the earlier, more unorthodox ideas from Malcolm Allison, he helped me to build a decent reputation as a coach. Wilf stated that if I was to become a first class manager, I had to obtain the highest qualifications, sufficient to talk to any other coach or athlete on equal terms. Over the years, he was proven to be absolutely right, and once I had received my Senior AAA badge in 1981, the status gave me the strength, confidence, and respect required to exercise my position.

I thoroughly enjoyed my years in coaching and never thought I would get even more satisfaction bringing success to others compared to my past personal sporting achievements. It was a great feeling when someone I had coached from scratch won an international vest or a major gold medal.

Among the many I have coached, two will remain in my memory. Liz Beeton, a rangy, determined, confident girl who won Junior 400 metre vests before settling for a medical career. Michelle Scutt (née Probert) was a totally different character, but immensely talented. When Michelle first came to Sale with her father, Phil, she favoured the shorter sprints, breaking the National Intermediate 200 metre record. She was persuaded to move up to 400 metres when she became the club's first Olympic medallist, winning bronze in the 1980 Moscow Olympics. She was also selected for the 1984 Los Angeles Olympics. In addition, she also won a silver 400 metre medal in the Commonwealth Games. To this day, I hear from both girls, who now have grown up children of their own and will always have fond memories and great pride at their success on the track.

Having proved ourselves in the Cheshire League, in 1973 we were elected to the Second Division of the Motorway League, which consisted of major clubs situated close to the motorway system. We won promotion in our first year of membership and in the second year came a most respectable third in the First Division.

The Northern Track and Field League was formed in 1973, whose purpose was to give competition to clubs in the north of England not involved with national competition. Three age groups were included, Junior (Under 15s), Intermediate (Under 17s), and Seniors. Sale ('B' team) was elected to the First Division. Well known athletes who were selected for the National League teams were not permitted to participate, this giving our fringe members necessary competition at a decent level. Over twenty-nine years (no league in 1976), we won the Championship seventeen times and were unbeaten until the change to Seniors in 1994. It is now recognised as the North of England Track and Field League. I was involved in the original formation of the league and acted as chairman for many years.

In 1975 the UK League was formed, covering all age groups, that is, Under 15s, Under 17s and Seniors, with joint scoring. Four divisions each of six clubs were proposed, with teams taken from all areas of Great Britain. Surprisingly, we were elected to the First Division and have remained there since, being the only club ever over the past thirty years to have retained premiership status.

In our first season we achieved runners-up to Edinburgh Southern, who won the inaugural UK League title. The following year, in 1976, we collected our first First Division championship and repeated this distinction in 1977 and 1978 for the hat trick. Just before the coach left from Sale, a man stepped out of the crowd and presented me with a very large, green, red, and white elephant, the club colours, to bring us luck in Scotland. On the way up, my daughter, Lisa, dressed 'Harriet the Harrier', now our appointed mascot, in her Club vest and one of the other girls donated her shorts, and a hat was knitted in Sale colours en route. We won, and Harriet has terrorised clubs to this day with her presence, still wearing the original clothing.

I can vividly remember crying with emotion in the dressing room, overcome with the day's great success in beating the champions Edinburgh for the first time on their home soil with such a young squad. On that day the famous Sale team spirit was born and still exists in abundance.

3

There are so many stories relating to early years, and so many different personalities who have worn Sale Harrier colours. Parents can be a blessing, but some cannot see beyond their daughter's presence. A black girl in the Under 17 age group showed exceptional promise in sprinting and was a naturally gifted athlete. Following my principle of involving both the parents and schools, I discussed her potential with her father and her involvement at Sale. Thereafter there began a series of telephone calls from him during the early hours of the morning, always starting with, "Is that you white man?" Realising at once that he was trying to intimidate me, I played him at his own game, indicating that it was normal to discuss athletes at 6.30 a.m. in the morning. Gradually this did the trick, and when the season got on its way and his daughter was selected for the team, he became very awkward and would not agree to her running without his consent. As the first UK League fixture drew close, he eventually phoned, as usual, early morning, "Is that you white man? You have three League fixtures, my daughter will compete in two and I will decide which," then he hung up. At the last minute he agreed to allow her to run (she won convincingly), but with such pressure, she only lasted one further season.

I have always made sure that a young athlete got home safely after a match and have endured some nail biting moments when personally escorting girls to say the sixth floor of a high rise flat in the early hours of the morning. Nearly always I was followed to the door by a group of suspicious, local male residents who, in their own way, were ensuring the girls did not come to harm. Although my wife believed in the principle, she was always relieved when I arrived home in tact.

An eleven year old girl, whom I will call 'M', was spotted running for her school over cross country, so I obtained her address and decided to call at her home to discuss her potential with her parents. I arrived at the house to find all the windows were boarded up. I looked through a crack and saw that the living room was full of people of all ages. When a large Alsatian sat up in front of the television, it was duly pelted and ordered to lie down. I knocked at the front door, and suddenly there was silence; the room emptied at record speed. For a while, I stood outside, then suddenly M shouted from an upstairs window, "It's okay; it's only Mr Hughes," they thought it was the rent man! I spoke with her parents, and we agreed that I would collect M the following Sunday morning and take her to Sale for a training session. We arrived late, and as the group had already left for a run, I pointed M in the direction of the changing rooms and said I would follow on with her. After a few minutes she came out loaded with purses, cash, and various valuables and said to me, "Look what I've nicked," believing this was the right thing to do.

I sat down with her and explained why it was wrong and asked her how would she feel if someone had stolen her bus fare and she was unable to get home. We took the goods back to the changing room and placed them on a table and locked the door, giving the impression of a break in that had been discovered. M realised, when she made friends with the Sale girls, the wrong she had done. After I investigated the background of her large family, I found that all her brothers and sisters had been to jail and that nicking was a way of life. As time went on, M won many honours for her natural running talent, and this changed the whole family's attitude. They took great pride in her achievements. Her mother travelled on the club bus, and one of her brothers, fresh out of jail, made her a cabinet to display her medals. Unfortunately, as M grew older, in spite of all the support she received from the club training became a bind, but at least for a number of years she had travelled the country, seen a different way of life, and enjoyed her place in the sun.

On another occasion, to assist the men's team, I traced a very gifted high jumper, whom I will identify as 'A'. At school, he had shown exceptional promise as a natural athlete. In order to recruit him to Sale I eventually found his home in North Manchester and understood why he was a high jumper: the grass and weeds in his front garden were so tall, it would take an athlete to clear them. I knocked at the door and there was a blood curdling howl; I heard a voice shouting, "Shut up, Grumble." A long-haired youth, who appeared to be A, opened the door, holding back a massive, vicious, black hound who obviously wanted to get at me. Shaking, I introduced myself, and after explaining the purpose of my visit, I was invited inside, with Grumble straining at the leash. After sitting down on the settee, A explained that Grumble would behave provided I sat still, so with one eye on the brute, I gave the spiel on the Harriers and the benefits A would derive. During this time blood shot eyes (the dog's) never left me, but when A agreed to join, I produced an application form and handed him a pen to sign. With that movement Grumble exhausted his patience, broke free, and grabbed me by the wrist. But after the words, "Get down Grumble," I was released, complete with teeth marks, and decided to make my exit as soon as possible. A and Grumble saw me out (thankful to be alive), and as compensation, A proved himself to be an exceptional high jumper for both the club and his school, but without Grumble.

4

In 1979 we finished runners-up, and in 1980 we got off to a disastrous start when our coach was delayed on the motorway on our way to Bristol. Unfortunately, the meeting went ahead without us, and we missed a number of events. With insufficient time to warm up for others, we came in fifth. Despite winning the next match at Grangemouth convincingly, we came second in the final meeting and came in second overall.

In 1981, we lost the championship on match points only; 1982 saw us runners-up again. We were crowned champions again in 1983 and 1984, came in third in 1985, and won once more in 1986. The latter was a golden year when we achieved a treble of the UK League, the Senior Cross Country, and National Road Relay titles.

In 1987 we were again runners-up, and in 1988 came third. For the next two years, 1989–1990, we went unbeaten, and we also won the championship in 1991 and 1992. Harriet the Harrier was kidnapped by our close rivals at the time, Essex Ladies, who demanded that we concede the title to ensure her safe return! It was second once more in 1993 when I was paid the compliment of the Glasgow team throwing darts at an enlarged picture of me to generate team spirit—Glasgow won!

In 1991, I had the honour of being voted the first Sportsman of the Year for Trafford.

History was made in 1994 when the UK League changed its formation to become seniors only. Many believed that Sale would suffer, attributing our success to the strength of our younger athletes in the three tier system. We proved everyone outside the club wrong by winning the championship outright, dropping only one league point. We won again the following year in 1995 and made it a hat trick in 1996.

The one point we dropped was at Essex and with just one hour to go before the team's departure the telephone rang, Vicky Jenson, our 400 metre hurdler, had been stung by a bee and was on her way to the hospital. She was quite ill and obviously could not make the trip, which left us short in a difficult technical event, especially since the squad was already down to the bare bones.

One of the main objectives of a team manager is to fill every place, because history shows that matches are sometimes won by a single point, but to find someone to stand in for a 400 metre hurdles race seemed highly remote. The team always enjoyed a drink together at the hotel the night before, with the heavy throws athletes consuming more than others. I discreetly moved around, sounding out a possible volunteer, when Karen Brown, our hammer thrower, in a buoyant mood, said, "Put my name down, I'll have a go." After breakfast the next morning, an anxious Karen approached me saying, "I had a bad dream last night that I was going to run in the 400 metre hurdles today, but this can't be true." I replied, "Your dream will come true, you line up at 1.30 p.m. giving you ample time to recover from your selected event." With great credit a white faced, but courageous Karen duly took her place in the B event, passionately supported and applauded by her teammates. By kicking most of the hurdles down, she did not finish last. At the end of the day, we only lost by a mere two points. After the result was announced, I congratulated the opposing team manager, but told him that we had only been beaten by a bee!

The next three years, 1997 (4th), 1998 (4th), and 1999 (2nd) saw us consolidate, then from the turn of the century, from 2000 to 2004, we collected an unprecedented five successive UK League First Division titles, smashing the League points record on two occasions.

Overall, in thirty years we had then won eighteen titles; we were runners-up on seven occasions, placed third three times and fourth twice.

UK League positions over 30 years:

First 1976, 1977, 1978, 1983, 1984, 1986, 1989, 1990, 1991, 1992,
       1994, 1995, 1996, 2000, 2001, 2002, 2003, 2004
Second 1975, 1979, 1981, 1982, 1987, 1993, 1999
Third 1980, 1985, 1988,
Fourth 1997, 1998.

The idea of a Young Athletes League was originally introduced in 1990s as the Woolworth's Challenge Cup, consisting of the Under 15s and Under 17s age groups, based on three league matches and a Cup Final in September. We won the Cup for the first three years and came in third in 1993 when McDonald's became sponsors and were runners-up in 1994, 1995, 1997, 1998, and 2000, winning again in 1999. Since the inception of the League we have appeared in the final each year. UK Athletics took on sponsorship in 2002.

The National Track and Field Cup was first introduced in the late 1960s as an alternative to league competition. It was renamed the Jubilee Cup in 1977 to commemorate the Queen's Silver Anniversary. This was held in August/September each year with eight clubs participating in the final to decide the club representing Great Britain in Europe.

We qualified for the original competition in 1975 with a team comprising entirely teenagers, and as the structure was based on one senior per event, it took Sale some time to adjust.

However, the public witnessed some memorable moments on television when in 1977, one of our black athletes was leading her race when she stopped halfway on the track and threw her arms in the air when she heard over the loud speaker that Arthur Ashe had become the first black tennis player to win at Wimbledon.

Another time, I was horror stricken when an athlete slowed to straighten her bra strap in the middle of a 200 metre race, watched by millions.

I thought 1984 was going to be our first ever Cup victory, and we were leading with just the 4 x 400 metres relay to go. We were ahead at the final lap, but a young unknown girl ran out of her skin and crossed the line to be eventually given the verdict by one hundredth of a second, after six photo finish checks. The girl's name was Sally Gunnell.

On the occasion of one semi-final at Luton, traditionally held on a Sunday, our number one high jumper called off injured on the prior Saturday morning. Next in line was Beverley Howarth, who lived in Darwen, and I continually tried to contact her by phone, without success. As time progressed, I said to my wife, "Do you fancy a trip out to Darwen for lunch?" as apart from this being Bev's home, her family appeared to have a shop there. We eventually found the appropriate address, but the house was empty, and even after visiting the local police station, we could not find the shop. Returning to the house, I climbed over the back fence to see if there was any sign of life and was confronted by a neighbour who mistook me for a burglar. I was saved from embarrassment by the return of Bev's parents, who informed me that the family were leaving for a caravan holiday in Cornwall the following day, to which I responded, tongue in cheek, "Would you be passing Luton on the way?" After explaining the situation, they generously agreed to drop Bev off and wait until she had competed before continuing their journey. There was a happy ending to the story, as Bev cleared a personal best, winning maximum points, and she helped the team to victory. In athletics some parents can be a pain, but if they were to award gold medals for support, Bev's Mum and Dad would be one of the first on my list.

In 1998, after seventeen attempts, we eventually won the Cup, giving us our first taste of top European track and field competition the following year. It was traditional to throw the team manager in the water jump, and with this knowledge I quickly disappeared from sight. As an alternative there was a cry of "Let's get the elephant!" and poor Harriet was dunked into the water. There then followed the sight of the elephant being resuscitated with the kiss of life. Harriet was then stuffed into bin bags and when opening these at home the hall floor was flooded and it took a week to repair and dry out before Harriet was ready to take her place the following week for the Young Athletes Cup Final.

The next year we lost by the narrowest of margins, and I conducted tactics from my hospital bed while recovering just hours after an operation.

Back to the victory podium again in 2000, I persuaded the team not to repeat throwing Harriet in the water jump and hid her in the boot of my car. I returned to the track and was innocently told by the team that they would keep their word, but noticed they had dug a grave in the sandpit for a burial service.

Success continued in 2001 when we won the Cup by a record number of points and performances, which was also the last year of separate Men's and Women's competition.

In 2002, the club came third overall, and in 2003 runners-up. In 2004, a joint team was a disappointing sixth.

5

Two years after I had committed myself to athletics I attended a reunion of North Withington FC with whom I finished my soccer days. During the evening the Secretary of the Club asked me why I had turned to athletics and not continued my career in football. I replied that I wished to do something at national level in sport, but at the time never dreamed that my path would take me into such international circles, leading Sale into no fewer than thirty-five European contests over twenty-two years.

The overseas adventure began when, after winning the Senior National CC Championships, we were chosen to represent England in the inaugural 1982 European Clubs Cross Country Championships in Formia, Italy. After organising the trip, I had to miss out due to an important business commitment. Kath Binns took the individual bronze, but we were just beaten on the line by Italy for the gold medals; Portugal came in third, with the first three countries being elected as founder members. My daughter and son-in-law travelled with the team, and they said that when Elio Paponetti (the organiser) and myself met, there would be an explosion due to our similar outgoing personalities.

In 1983, the championships were held in Vertibo, Tuscany, the only residence that the Pope had ever lived apart from the Vatican. Upon arriving late, and after settling the team, I was whisked away in a gritty condition, unwashed and unshaven, to an unknown destination. This turned out to be a Civic reception, some miles from the hotel, and when I got there I was shown into a special room in the company of the other team managers and officials with no time for introductions.

After a short wait we were paraded into a large, brilliantly lit banqueting hall and shown to the top table, mixing with local mayors, highly decorated generals and well-attired special guests. Being very much aware of my scruffy appearance, I was placed in a VIP position (as runners-up in 1982) and was told that we were on national television. This was my very first personal encounter with Elio Paponetti, who went on air to begin proceedings in typical Italian fashion and then, to my amazement, I was invited in front of the cameras to be interviewed by a well-known journalist. In broken English he introduced me, not as Eric Hughes, but as 'Mr Sole Harrier' and asked if my club was capable of going one better than last year. Remembering what Malcolm Allison had told me years ago about positive speaking when in a corner, I took a very belligerent attitude and waved the Union Jack (verbally), in no uncertain manner, to rapturous applause with 'Bravo Sole Harrier'; it appeared that I was stuck with the name.

The following morning at the hotel I came across two famous Scottish athletes from different clubs and learned that they had travelled as the Scottish Union expecting to participate as a club which, of course, was not possible. This created a huge problem, because they had come a long way to compete and could be disqualified. Speaking to their team manager it would appear that the error was genuine, and I made a request for a meeting with Elio Paponetti to try to resolve the situation. He said he would meet me in one hour at a table in the corner of the dining room, ensuring that all the relevant officials would be present. When I arrived, I was surprised to see him sitting alone, and he said, "What is it you want?" I suggested that the Scottish girls should be allowed to run, but without team recognition. He replied his now famous words, "Okay, I fix," and the race went ahead on these lines.

In spite of my bravado, Sale had to be content with team bronze medals, but we produced the very first individual British winner in Katherine Carter. On the course after the race, the same TV character from the previous evening grabbed me and 'Katrina', as she was christened, and once more I appeared on national TV as 'Mr Sole Harrier' and was widely acknowledged wherever I went.

During the early evening, a meeting of the various countries was held to constitute a committee, and Elio Paponetti immediately stated that he would be President. When it came to the second nomination, in spite of our 'conflicts', I was amazed when he said, "There is only one person for Vice President, and that is 'Mr Sole Harrier'." Later I put the record straight and I was registered as Eric Hughes, and so began a strong relationship of working together to expand European Club Cross Country competition, and our friendship exists until today.

To mark the occasion, catacombs in a nearby village were opened after many years and converted into a banqueting suite. The atmosphere was unique, with candlelit tables and a famous opera singer from Rome for entertainment. In true Italian style, the award ceremony was a glittering, but long, drawn-out affair. Katrina was very popular, and once again we were interviewed together by the same journalist. A trophy was presented to each country that had taken part, and England received an enormous cup in bronze and marble, standing over two feet high and weighing a 'ton'. The catacombs were in an isolated position, about half a mile from transport, and after the festivities ended, it took at least two people to carry the trophy, which was now proving to be an embarrassment. Staggering through cobbled streets accompanied by hysterical giggles from local women shouting, "Ciao," hanging out of their windows as we passed. The following morning, I decided that something had to be done to lose the thing, but as we were accompanied to the airport, I had to check it in. On going through the departure lounge, I was stopped by an American who said, "If that held the egg, what must the chicken have been like?" On the homeward journey the thing attracted plenty of attention, and when I eventually arrived at the doorstep of my home, my wife, who has a calm disposition, exclaimed, "What on earth is that?"

A civic reception had been arranged at the Trafford Town Hall in our honour. After I had acknowledged a speech by the Mayor, I arranged for one of our male hammer throwers to bring the thing to the presentation area and gave it to the Council in return for their recognition and generosity. At last I thought it was gone from my life, but a year later I received a telephone call from the Town Hall to collect it. Our Secretary at the time, Harold Wilson, came to the rescue and said that he would use it in his garden to keep plants in. *Arrivederci* the thing!

The 1984 Championship was again held in Italy, this time in Cassino in the shadow of the famous monastery, and the team came in third once more, with a reported sixty million TV viewers watching. Three of the team members, including Diane Edwards, were still at school, all aged seventeen years, and to win bronze medals from the sixteen nations that took part was no mean achievement. Katherine Carter again was our top scorer in third place. When the Harriers arrived on the course in their green, red and white tracksuits, they were mistaken for the Italians as these are the colours of their national flag. A large number of spectators, which included coach loads of schoolchildren, continuously shouted, "Italia, Italia," and did not find out until later that they were supporting the wrong team.

Transport was coordinated by the Italian army and we had no less than a general to supervise our movements. A tour of Rome was organised on the Sunday before our departure. All went well until our coach got caught up in heavy traffic, giving us little time to reach the airport. However, our arrogant general appeared totally unperturbed, saying there was no need to panic, in spite of one of the girls continually nagging him, knocking his hat off twice, as it was essential she returned home on schedule. As we approached the Rome airport, our plane had just taken off; the confident general mistook the departure time for check in. The Italian airport officials said that we could not use our tickets for an alternative flight as special rates had been agreed and it would cost about £350 per person to get back to Manchester.

Our now subdued general was a subject of embarrassment, and I nominated three of our strongest girls to hold on to him, one on each leg and one clutching his body. This was to ensure he did not escape while I telephoned Elio Paponetti. In due course, he reprimanded the general in no uncertain manner and arranged for us to have overnight accommodations at a nearby seaside hotel and then fly off early the following Monday morning.

Spain hosted the tournament in 1985. The venue was about twenty kilometres from Madrid, and although the team came in a disappointing sixth, we were gaining valuable experience all the time. Great preparations had taken place to create a carnival atmosphere before the race, with a huge crowd, band performances, and parachute drops, but the organisers had neglected one very important factor—toilets. With our girls dying to go, I suggested they form a close circle and each went in turn in the centre. The idea caught on and with little delay all the twenty participating countries copied the idea and the large warm-up area was littered with 'relief circles' in different coloured tracksuits.

We travelled to the Algarve in Portugal in 1986 with a depleted team; four of our stars out of six were missing, and we came in a not unexpected tenth.

However, 1987 in Clusone, Italy, was a completely different story. In spite of losing Kath Carter with a pulled hamstring at the last minute, we came back with a bang and collected the team silver medals. The setting was in the mountains, some ninety kilometres east of Milan, on an icy, treacherous, 5300 metre course. Sue Crehan led the team home. The second counter was the newly crowned Commonwealth 800 metre silver medallist, Diane Edwards, quite a contrast in distance, climate, and conditions.

When we arrived in the area the day before, we were somewhat disappointed not to be staying at the main hotel in the town, but about fifteen kilometres out in a small, private lodge. As it happened, this was not a bad thing, as we were comfortable, warm, and relieved when we heard that the main hotel was without water. As usual a coach was allocated to each nation, with a guide/interpreter, and on the morning of our departure we were the starting point, working our way to the main hotel to collect the Irish, Scottish, and Welsh Men's teams who were booked on similar flights back to the UK. We arrived to find the hotel surrounded by soldiers, and pushing my way into the foyer, I was told that the hotel had blamed the British contingency for damage done to furniture and mirrors the previous night, and that they would not be allowed to leave until they had paid compensation. As the team managers had refused to do this, the Italian army had been called in.

With one eye on the clock, I sorted out the relevant team managers, who agreed that some of their athletes had run riot, but would not take the blame. I told them that they should have a whip round of all concerned and pay the hotel manager his dues. I also told them that we would wait half an hour for them to appear, otherwise the coach would leave without them. In twenty-five minutes three disgruntled parties boarded the coach after acceding to my suggestion, and we all caught the homeward flights from Milan on time.

Wales did Britain proud by hosting the 1988 Championships in Cardiff, but there was controversy about a rule adjustment declaring three, and not four, athletes to score. The invited nations were paraded through the streets of Cardiff behind a colourfully dressed Welsh Guards band, complete with their goat mascot, to reach the historical course set around Cardiff castle. This included a run along the battlements. We came a close fourth, and the girls were well turned out, as usual, for the presentation banquet in the evening, presided over by the Lord Mayor.

6

In 1989, we returned to the Algarve, where we came fifth from the ever increasing fierce opposition. Portugal had won everything in sight. Beverley Nicholson was late leaving London and missed her connecting flight to Manchester. Although our take off to Lisbon was delayed, we left the ground as Bev's plane was landing in Manchester. By using the pilot's on board telephone, I made tentative arrangements for her to follow, and after catching a later flight, she arrived in Lisbon just as the airport was closing on the wrong side of Portugal. A distressed Bev contacted me at our Algarve headquarters, saying she had no local currency and no idea what to do. I told her to find a taxi and that I would settle with the driver whenever they arrived. During the early hours of the morning, a furious, frustrated Bev drove up, still cursing British Airways for not waiting for her, and yet the following day she ran out of her skin and became our top scorer. Upon our return to Manchester, she stormed into a British Airways Executive meeting still very angry. She received an apology and free flights for the next year.

Braga in Northern Portugal was next selected for the 1990 tournament, the home of the reigning champions. The race was run in monsoon conditions in ankle deep mud. Two of our girls were injured on the course, so we did well to finish in sixth position. Our hosts made the award presentations in a very ordinary fashion, not the usual banquet. To compensate, they gave each team free passes to a nightclub adjacent to the hotel. When we arrived a six-foot, leather clad, black go-go dancer was doing her stuff on the stage, and our two petite, blonde bombshells decided they could do better. Sue Parker and Janice Moody, complete with a strapless dress and long, white gloves, took over and did their stuff to such applause that the audience would not let them leave to allow the professional dancer to resume. As the night drew on it became apparent that drugs were being taken in abundance and, as the atmosphere became dangerous, we struggled to take our leave.

I was prevented from attending the 1991 Championships, which were held in San Remo in thick snow. In 1992, we returned to Cassino, Italy, with the team again coming in sixth over a gruelling 6300 metre course with a record twenty-one nations taking part.

A Russian team made history by appearing, for the first time, without the usual KGB escort. They had no experience of overseas club competition, and they seemed like ducks out of water. Our girls befriended the athletes, and Barry Wilkinson and myself looked after the coach with the aid of a Russian vocabulary. The bond grew between us, and after the presentation banquet we had retired for the night in preparation for an early start the following morning. But before too long, a knock came at my door. There stood the coach, and in broken English exclaimed, "We party." After dressing, and waking the others, we made our way to the Russian section of the hotel to discover that they had removed the furniture from one room and invited us in. The coach produced a bottle of vodka, Barry brought a bottle of Scotch, and we were still together celebrating until the early hours.

During the proceedings Suzanne Rigg (6th) and Larissa Emlianenko (8th) kept glancing at each other, and suddenly the Russian girl appeared to remember something, went to her room, and returned with a tee shirt identifying a top road race held in Carolina, USA, a couple of months back. This clicked with Suzanne and they realised they had both competed in that same race, finishing close together. So Larissa had travelled from Moscow, Suzanne from Manchester, meeting up in Italy after running against each other in America—some coincidence!

The very first Women's Russian Steeplechase had taken place the previous autumn, and the inaugural champion was with us in the hotel room. We decided that we would make a special gesture to mark the occasion and presented her with a Club vest on condition that whenever she wore it she would say, "Sale Harriers fantastic." She learned this in English and kept repeating the expression until she knew it by heart.

The following year in the Algarve, the famous Almond Blossom race was held before the European Championships. I noticed there was a girl on the starting line in a Sale vest, but was puzzled as to whom she could be. Shortly after the race began I was standing with Barry at the side of the course when she ran over to us and shouted, "Sale Harriers fantastic." Guess who!

Elio Paponetti was reelected President and myself Vice President of the European Clubs Cross Country Committee. After ten years, the competition was recognised as a major European fixture.

As mentioned, we returned yet again to the Algarve in 1993, this time in Albufeira, where we finished seventh; in 1994, Cassino was specially chosen once more to mark the fiftieth anniversary of the famous monastery siege. During the war, the Germans held out there for three months, despite being bombarded by the Allies, and many lives were lost.

On the Saturday morning, Elio Paponetti asked me to gather the other team managers together and meet on the town hall steps at 10.00 hours. This appeared to be for the usual civic reception, but when we arrived, hundreds of people filled the adjacent square and a band in all its finery was playing away. As we were waiting on the steps, Elio suddenly appeared with the mayor and a good number of well-known local dignitaries. He thrust a large wreath in my arms and said, "You lead." I was placed behind the band, who had now lined up in formation, and with the other team managers just behind, we marched through the crowded streets of Cassino on national television to the cemetery where I laid the wreath on a newly built memorial. It would have been nice to have had some warning of the occasion, but in any event it was something to be part of the history I had only read about at school.

There was no competition in 1995 and the championship was held in 1996 in Lanciano on the Adriatic side of Italy. The principle memory I have of that is travelling through an electric storm over the mountains.

In 1997, Wales was again the venue, this time in Newport. With two days of heavy rain, the course was flooded, but somehow the race went ahead.

We did not participate in the 1998 Championship in Istanbul, but I was commissioned to travel there to maintain our home countries' rights to compete. Since the inception of the tournament England, Ireland, Scotland and Wales had been permitted to enter teams, but a number of European nations had objected to this, stating there should be representation by one team only from Great Britain. As we held independent championships in the UK, this would not be possible, and my brief was to meet members of the European Committee and convince them that all four countries should continue. After three days of debate and wining and dining, aided by the fact that in addition to England both Scotland and Wales would be soon functioning under independent rule, I eventually convinced the powers enough for them to reconsider. Later I heard that I had managed to win the case.

Due to heavy commitments, I decided to resign my Vice Presidency. This was at first rejected by Elio Paponetti, who organised the next annual conference to be held in Manchester in October 2000, close to where I lived, making it impossible for me not to attend. In spite of the circumstances, the committee had a most enjoyable weekend. It was a pleasure to entertain Elio and his colleagues in Manchester. However, the ploy did not work, and I stuck to my decision to retire from the committee.

In 1999, 2000, and 2001, we did not compete, but again, after winning the domestic National Championships, we travelled to Bilbao in Spain in 2002. My personal reason for making the journey was to renew acquaintances with Elio Paponetti, but upon my arrival it was a great shock to learn that he had suffered a stroke and was partially paralysed. This would have been a tremendous blow to a normal person, but to a man of such energy, power and enthusiasm it was an appalling disaster. I will always treasure my friendship with Elio who achieved such incredible feats as persuading the Pope to start a race and organising a road race around Red Square in Moscow. Thankfully today, he has partially recovered, and I am still in touch with him.

Malcolm Allison 1971 Watching Lisa (right) and Stephen (left) During Ban
(By Courtesy of Manchester Evening News)

Eric and Bill One Of Athletics Most Successful Partnerships

Left to right:

Harold Wilson - *Sale Harriers Manchester Secretary.*
Gave 70 years service to the Club.

Katherine Binns - *World 10,000 metre record holder.*

Michelle Scutt - *The first member of Sale Harriers to win an Olympic medal.*

Eric Hughes

Eric With Kath Carter 1986 Winning All Major Trophies In One Year

Cup Winning Team 2001 With Harriet

Team Preparing European CC Cup 1982 On Beach At Formia, Italy

Eric With Paponetti 1990 Braga

Eric With Michelle Wilkinson (right) And Shelley Holroyd (left)
Track And Field Captains With 1989 European Cup

Diane Modahl (0306 Gold) Anne Williams (0371 Silver)
800 Metres 1990 Commonwealth Games, Auckland
(By Courtesy of Mark Shearman)

Eric 2008 With Trophy Collection

7

Backtracking to 1986, the European Juniors (Under 20s) Track and Field Cup was initiated, and by the method of a paper match, Sale Harriers won the rights to represent Great Britain in the inaugural meeting in Liege, Belgium, in October. This was late, because the Continent always have a rest from competition in August and then resume again in September to early October. The format is a definite disadvantage to UK sport. Most of our athletes have passed their best form by then, because generally we have concluded our season early to mid September each year.

With Bill Nicholls by my side, we decided to fly to Brussels and then journey on by coach, but due to various delays, the team had not eaten and arrived in Liege famished. While waiting for our local transport, the only alternative we had was to devour beefburgers in a local square. When our hosts eventually arrived, we were informed that the proposed sponsors had pulled out and that we would have to make do with limited facilities. We travelled about ten kilometres from town to find that the accommodations consisted of a wooden scout hut on an isolated hill, with one bunk house to take three nations (average twenty persons) and only one toilet. When we shook the blankets in our rooms, spiders emerged, and the entire situation was far from the international standards we had expected.

No dining facilities existed, but we were informed that a new sponsor had been found and that we would be driven into town for dinner that evening. This cheered everybody considerably, and the girls duly changed into their finery for the occasion. It was a beautiful evening;

the town looked inviting, but when our transport stopped in the centre we were each handed a voucher for a beefburger and one drink to use in a nearby McDonald's who were now our sponsors. Imagine the sight of fifteen well-dressed girls perched on a wall outside McDonald's in the centre of the town, eating beefburgers for the second time that day.

Saturday morning breakfast consisted of bread and margarine with lukewarm coffee. Because transport was at a premium, we had to leave early for the track. The agreed practice was for the host country to supply a packed lunch for each of the athletes, but to our horror, we discovered that beefburgers were again on the menu, provided by our sponsors McDonald's. This was too much, and I commissioned one of our coaches to find a supermarket or something similar in the vicinity to search for food and drink. He returned with fresh bread and orange juice to provide a more healthy lunch.

In spite of our problems the girls took everything in their stride, and we came in an excellent second to the German team, who had travelled in style and had stayed at a good hotel nearby. For our very young squad, it was a great honour to represent Great Britain and an experience for them to carry the Union Jack in a march past. Our position qualified us for the next Cup Final.

At an executive meeting after the match, I was elected vice president. I left Bill in charge and made my way overnight in fog to Birmingham to attend a UK League meeting on the Sunday to receive the First Division trophy,

There was no competition in 1987, but in 1988 we were invited to Rennes in France, travelling via Paris. After landing and taking the metro from the airport to Grand Central station, three of the girls took the wrong underground turn and finished up a good distance outside the city. We waited for hours before they were able to join us after posting lookouts at each exit and entry point at the station. Our scheduled train had left a considerable time before and we boarded a slow, all night excursion, arriving at a deserted Rennes station in the early hours of the morning.

Once again the team performed out of their skins. With six of our athletes only sixteen years old, we collected no fewer than eleven individual medals. We held a winning position with just the 4 x 100 metres relay to go. We had better sprinters than Hungary, our nearest rivals, and we were well ahead after the first leg, then disaster struck. Our outgoing athlete took the baton perfectly, but inexplicably dropped it mid way on the second takeover and by the time she had recovered the baton it was too late. We came in an inevitable last with just one point, meaning we had forfeited the anticipated ten points, losing the match by four points. The athlete concerned was heartbroken, and despite the support she received from everybody there was little we could do to console her. The incident was totally out of character. So ended our dream of being the first club to win a major European Cup, and we vowed we would return the next year and make amends.

On the return journey home, due to a misunderstanding of the clock change, no transport arrived at the hotel on the Sunday morning. We ordered emergency taxis, and we just caught the connecting train for Paris, sprinting down the platform with only seconds to spare.

Paris in fact was the setting for the 1989 Cup Final, and this was also the year of the Manchester Olympic bid, making our trip even more significant. To highlight the occasion, the Olympic Committee agreed to fund our air fares. With the media in abundance, a cheque was presented at the airport. Amid all the hullabaloo and publicity it was not until after take off that I realised that the cheque was blank, a situation not rectified until some months later.

On the big day, we fulfilled our promise of the previous year and became the first British club to win a European Track and Field Championship, but not without plenty of drama. Our close rivals were again Budapest from Hungary. Toward the end of the meeting, we appeared to be destined for another runners-up spot, being thirteen points in arrears with just five events to go. Two consecutive victories and a second place brought us level, with just the two relays to go. Both countries shared the honours; we dead heated with 167 points each.

As the trophy had to be won outright, a jury consisting of the senior officials present was formed and retired for coffee and cognac. Some time later, with me pacing up and down the track looking like an expectant father, the jury disclosed that the team with the greatest number of gold medals would be declared the winner. On count back both Sale and Budapest had achieved four gold medals each and the jury retired once again. After another agonising, lengthy interval, the jury agreed that the cup would be won by the greater number of silver medals. Sale had collected four, and Hungary only two, so the trophy was on its way to Great Britain. For a team so young (average age seventeen-and-a-half years) they deserved great credit for their remarkable composure and competitive spirit, particularly as the Eastern bloc countries had virtually fielded their national sides. With such excitement and tension I was in quite a state, but the most patient man in the stadium, Bill Nicholls, calmly smoked his pipe at the back of the stand and took everything philosophically.

The hosts arranged a grand banquet for the presentations. As we entered the large hall, we received a standing ovation, but due to a mix up, no table was available for us. The new European champions then enjoyed their meal sitting cross legged on the floor.

Earlier in the evening, I had telephoned my wife to tell her the good news and also to find out the result of the Manchester soccer derby held that afternoon. I was told the score was 5–1; when I asked who had got City's goal, I was informed that City had won, scoring five in another memorable match.

One of my fondest memories was the following Sunday when we enjoyed a celebratory trip down the Seine, with a relieved me clutching the Cup at the back of the boat, bathed in warm sunshine. We received a wonderful welcome back at Manchester airport, with Harriet the Harrier in attendance.

As cup holders, we were asked to host the 1990 meeting in Manchester, resulting in one of the most stressful times in my life. We had no stadium as such in Wythenshawe Park, but with the help of the council, we arranged to have a temporary stand built, together with portable toilets. Gilbert Everard, the European secretary, later inspected the site on an exploratory visit. Even though he had to relieve himself in the bushes at the time of his visit, he left with a promise that there would be suitable facilities provided on the day.

There was also the huge question of finance as a large amount of money would have to be raised to meet the expense of accommodating, catering to, and entertaining the expected sixteen participating nations.

We had to arrange a formal banquet, and trophies and medals had to be commissioned for each team. After due consideration, we decided to go ahead and form a subcommittee to organise the event, with mid-September in mind.

The search for funding began, and it was obvious from the start that a major sponsor was out of the question. We came up with the idea of inviting separate sponsors at a cost of £1000 for each team and a trophy engraved with their name to be presented at the farewell banquet in person by one of their executives. The idea worked, and this solved a huge financial problem.

Manchester Airport, who were the Club's principal sponsors at the time, were first in line and also supplied local transport over the three days of the event. The nearby Posthouse at Northenden gave us an attractive rate when we took over the entire hotel, and various local traders chipped in with packed lunches, drinks, the use of walkie talkies, and so forth. We received useful individual donations as well. In addition to the track facilities, Manchester City Council recognised the importance of the event and allowed us to use the Great Hall at the Town Hall for the banquet, together with adjacent rooms for reception and entertaining.

There was still a busy Track and Field season to get through, but we still managed to win the UK League and the Young Athletes Cup by the end of August. The pressure increased daily, and some weeks before the meeting I lost two key members of the Committee with stress breakdowns. I was virtually left alone with additional business commitments to meet and struggled night and day to cope. I must have been impossible to live with at the time and will never forget my wife's support and tolerance and how it affected our home life. At this stage, I remembered that the French team manager the previous year had worn a smart, white suit at the evening banquet. When I remarked on his appearance he told me this was his wedding outfit from twenty years ago and that he had never been able to get into it until now. This was due to the loss of weight from the worry of organising the European Cup, and I knew exactly what he meant.

As the day drew nearer, the Stalker family came to the rescue and took over the catering, other club members lent a hand, and we welcomed the incoming overseas countries to Manchester on the Friday, praying for good weather the following day. This was not to be, however; when I woke up on Saturday, the rain was torrential and never stopped. Marquees had been erected and the temporary stand was packed with VIPs who had come to witness the first ever European Clubs Cup held in the UK. All the prethought and detailed planning paid off, and thanks to a team of hardworking top Track and Field officials, the match went to time. This proved to be a ding-dong battle between Sale and Yugoslavia. In spite of us winning three gold, three silver, and five bronze medals, we had to settle for second place. Marea Hartman, who was at the time President of the AAA, sought me out later indicating that she believed three of the Yugoslavian team members were over age. She promised that when she returned to her office after the weekend, she would check this out. Marea proved to be right, and Sale were robbed of the trophy which was never returned and from that day onwards, each country are required to produce passports to check the validity of their athletes.

Under the circumstances, the athletic side of the meeting was a big success, and the banquet afterwards in the town hall is still remembered as the best ever. Over 300 people sat down for dinner within an amazing setting in the Great Hall. The top table consisted of the sponsors, team managers, and just two speakers, John Stalker, our Chairman at the time, and the Lord Mayor. Everyone who had played a part had been invited, including a special table for the officials. Formality was kept to a minimum, and the atmosphere was magnificent. Other guests joined us afterwards for a disco, with nationalities from all over Europe mingling and enjoying themselves. Once it was over, I was immensely relieved and totally exhausted. Although the occasion had taken a lot out of my wife and myself, at least we had the satisfaction of a job well done—but never again!

8

We returned again to Paris in 1991 and won the cup convincingly for the second time from the Polish team. I was awarded a prize for the best manager, which consisted of standing on a large scale at the presentation banquet and receiving my weight in Coca Cola. What do you do with hundreds of cans of Coca Cola on a Saturday evening in Paris? We distributed these to the security guards and various helpers, but retained a case in the boot of the team bus for later consumption.

Instead of a disco, the organisers came up with the idea of hiring boats for a trip down the Seine, but unfortunately our coach got lost on the way to the terminal and the boat left without us. Last time we won there was no table for us at the banquet and now this; perhaps this is the way the French treat champions! We had no alternative but to return to our hotel to drink the Coca Cola, but the boot of the coach got stuck and we were deprived of not only our liquid prize, but the gifts and trophies we had been given.

A record number of nineteen countries took part in the 1992 contest, held in Turin, Italy. This was dominated by Eastern bloc countries such as Eastern Germany, Czechoslovakia, Poland, and the Ukraine, who virtually fielded their national squads. We did very well to finish fifth, ahead of the other Western European teams and three of our athletes travelled half way across the globe from the World Junior Championship in Korea to support the Club.

The best route to reach Turin from Manchester was to fly to Milan direct and hire a coach to take us on and everything went to plan until we reached Turin.

We gave the driver the appropriate address for registration, but when we got there we were diverted to a shop across town occupied by members of the host club. There they explained to us that the intended sponsors were actually the local town council, but they had been locked up on a charge of conspiracy and sponsorship support had been abolished. Apparently the athletic meeting would go ahead on schedule, but the main problem was accommodation. In this respect, we were informed, "You British like the countryside," and we were loaded onto a coach and taken some twenty kilometres away to the middle of nowhere.

Our destination was a farmhouse with huge, iron gates, and the scene inside the courtyard was quite picturesque, with hens and ducks and other small animals flitting about. I told the girls to hang on to their belongings and asked the coach driver to wait while I checked out the accommodation. Thank heavens I did because the rooms consisted of dusty, large closets with bunks for three and no other space. Even so there was worse to come when I discovered the toilet facilities consisted of a hole in the ground with a shower alongside. This was open-plan for all to see, confirmed by the Russian men's team already leering down from the first floor. It was impossible for us to remain, so I assembled the team with their baggage and arranged for them to wait outside the gates until I returned. The driver of the coach spoke a little English, so I asked him to return to base.

After complaining, I learned that the Turkish team had not yet arrived and had been allocated a small hotel in the city. Boarding the coach, I accompanied the driver to the airport and welcomed the Turks, then directed them to the farmhouse. Seeing them off the bus our girls quickly climbed on board and we made our way to the city hotel, which was more than adequate. The next day, I dreaded meeting the Turkish manager. When I nervously asked him about the accommodations at the farmhouse, much to my relief, he indicated that it was fantastic. Possibly this was a case of what they were used to!

In 1993 we had to withdraw due to lack of finances required to make the trip to Slovenia, but in 1994 we again returned to Paris and completed a hat trick of European Junior Cups in the French capital.

Our lucky streak deserted us in 1995 when we only came in fourth, and in 1996 we had to withdraw at a late stage from the Bordeaux meeting, again because of the lack of finance. Due to this unfortunate situation I was honour bound to resign as vice president of the Committee.

Relegation followed to the Second Division, but in 1997 we won our spurs back by finishing runners-up to France in Amsterdam. Then, due to a change of rules, we were prevented from competing for four years.

Over the past three decades and more I have played some part in the lives of many athletes, but one stands out in my memory.

Diane Edwards (Modahl) joined Sale Harriers as an eleven-year-old some twenty-eight years ago. She had been spotted by top middle-distance coach, Alan Robertshaw, who recognised her potential in a school's race. Alan nurtured her obvious talent and encouraged Diane in her early years. I was there, as team manager, from day one to her eventual retirement from athletics.

As a youngster Diane was very successful in cross country and road running, winning a hat full of medals with the club. It became apparent that her track discipline would be the 800 metres, reflecting her natural speed and endurance.

Three times she was runner-up in the All England Schools, and in 1984 finally won the title in a record-breaking time, being awarded a Great Britain Junior vest at the age of sixteen years. In 1985, Diane collected her first senior British honours and won the silver medal at the Edinburgh Commonwealth Games in 1986, later breaking the two minute barrier for the first time at the Bislett games in Norway. Diane made the final of the Seoul Olympics in 1988 and won the Commonwealth gold medal in 1990 in Auckland with team mate Ann Williams (Griffiths) coming in second and doing the Club proud.

Looking forward to defending her title in Victoria, Canada, in 1994 Diane ran in a low key meeting in Lisbon during June and then secured a maximum eight points in the European Cup at Birmingham which led to Great Britain qualifying for the final. Both these meetings were to have a distinct effect on Diane's life.

August arrived and I was seated at home with my wife awaiting the 800 metre semi-final of the 1994 Commonwealth Games, looking forward to the first stage of Diane, as favourite, retaining her gold medal. I was mystified when her lane was left empty and no explanation was given for this at the time of the broadcast. However, later in the evening, I was shocked to hear that Diane had been withdrawn from the race because she had failed a drug test and was being flown back to England that very night.

When more information came to hand, it would appear that this was related to a test held in Lisbon some nine weeks beforehand, but only given to the English team manager by fax just before the start of the race in Victoria. The shock was so great that Diane collapsed, totally distraught, and was bundled on to an overnight flight to London, being met on arrival by husband Vicente and then retreating to a secret hotel hideaway. Early the following day my telephone line was red hot as I was besieged with calls from the media. My home and office were the centre of attraction for television, radio, and newspaper reporters. At one time there were three television crews and six reporters outside my office, all waiting for interviews.

Apart from a brief call from Vicente I had no concrete facts available and quickly had to reach a decision on Diane's innocence. Having a longstanding knowledge of Diane's integrity and her religious beliefs, I came to the instant conclusion that, irrespective of the circumstances, she could not be guilty of drug abuse and made this public. Diane later told me that one of the first television images she saw from her secret London hotel room was me supporting her cause, stating that she had done nothing wrong, and this gave her extra strength to carry on. Apart from my belief, the whole situation just did not add up, not least the nine week delay from the Lisbon meeting to the Commonwealth Games. Diane had proved negative in previous drug tests, there had been no drastic improvement in her performances, and no change in her appearance that would be noticeable if she had taken the massive dose of testosterone indicated.

Then a political story broke when it was reported in Russia that a British athlete had been found positive *weeks before* the announcement had been made in Victoria. The points scored by Diane in the European Cup had contributed to the Russians being eliminated by two points and if Diane were to be banned and disqualified they would qualify for the final in place of Great Britain. As expected the media made the most of this and I received calls from reporters in Russia, Stockholm, and all over Europe. In one instance, I was contacted by a source who claimed to be working in an official government capacity and for the purpose of identification I was given the code name 'Cobra'. The telephone would ring and a voice would say, "Cobra," and in return I had to repeat 'Cobra' three times before dialogue. My wife found it hilarious when I would pick up the phone exclaiming, "Cobra, Cobra, Cobra!", but without any real evidence the story eventually died down.

Even so, with the B test confirmed late August the British Athletic Federation had, under pressure, to determine whether Great Britain should compete in the European Cup Final at Crystal Palace in September. To their credit they decided not to withdraw on the lines that Diane was innocent until proven guilty. With this in mind, all kinds of theories emerged; 'Had the sample in Lisbon been stored correctly?', 'Had a drink been spiked?' A hearing was set in London for mid-December to review the case.

Meanwhile I was constantly supporting Diane through the media and was part of the Brendan Pittaway investigation for the BBC. In one instance the cameras turned up late at night at my home and I was interviewed in a floodlit sun lounge which became the setting in countries all over the world. On one occasion, the BBC felt that a programme from the track where Diane trained would be a good idea and decided on a live broadcast. This was set for 6.30 p.m. on a summer's evening, and when I reported at Wythenshawe Park half an hour beforehand, the full works were in swing. However, a problem occurred when the high trees surrounding the track prevented the signal into the Manchester studio, even though the camera tower was moved several times. Time was ticking on and I overheard the producer shout, "For .... sake, get him to the studio quickly!" I then followed a sports car at breakneck speed, red lights and all, down Princess Parkway and shot into a reserved parking spot under the BBC building on Oxford Road. There was no time to summon a lift, and I hurried up two flights of stairs accompanied by a make-up lady doing her stuff and sat down breathlessly next to the presenter with one minute to go. Whether it was the effects of adrenaline or spontaneous thinking, I was complimented afterwards for an impressive interview.

On another occasion, I went to the BBC studios by Metro to avoid parking and afterwards descended into Oxford Road forgetting to remove my make-up, and was promptly picked up by a gay passerby!

The BAF disciplinary hearing duly took place in London on 13 December 1994, but unfortunately the case was lost, in spite of heavy legal costs. Diane spoke publicly, again declaring her innocence, stating she would not accept the decision and would take matters to the Independent Appeal Panel.

Sale Harriers supported Diane by withdrawing from the European Cross Country Championships; it was bizarre that these were to be held in Portugal the following year after the incident in Lisbon. We had competed in these championships for thirteen consecutive years, and although it was disappointing for the athletes concerned, everyone in the club agreed with the action taken.

Early in 1995 a series of new scientific tests took place, and investigators revealed that the samples taken in Lisbon had been poorly stored, providing a dramatic increase in testosterone caused by bacteria. With this evidence, an appeal date was set for July and Diane was at last cleared.

On a brighter note Diane gave birth to a lovely daughter, Imani, in October 1995 and began training again. She finished her career with Sale Harriers by being part of the gold medal team that won the National Cross Country Championships in March 1996.

Humorously, someone suggested that a film be made on the saga with Whitney Houston as Diane, Arnold Schwarzenegger portraying Vicente and, wait for it, Walter Matthau playing me!

9

We represented Great Britain at the Senior European Clubs Championship in 1999 as the Jubilee Cup winners and made our debut in Athens. In spite of one gold, two silver, and one bronze individual medals we had to be content with eighth place. It was a case of taking on what were virtually national teams operating as clubs, allowed by the difference in rules for the opposing countries who could also field guest athletes at short notice. The contest was awesome, and additionally we had to cope with considerable stress due to the political situation in the Middle East, being victimised on and off the field of competition.

I had been invited to Seville the same weekend to earmark the World Cup, and Manchester City were at Wembley for the Second Division play offs, but could only be in one place at one time. As our match in Athens was nearing conclusion, Barry Wilkinson, also a passionate City supporter like myself, realised it was getting close to the final whistle at Wembley. After some difficulty with phone cards, Barry eventually got through to his wife to be told that City were one goal down with very little time to go, then he was cut off. Climbing back to a bar on top of the huge Olympic Stadium, he spoke again to home, then appeared down the tunnel of the track saying City had equalised and were playing a nail biting extra time.

Meanwhile I was organising the 4 x 400 metres squad (we recorded a club record), while Barry was seeking more news. When I looked up, I saw this small figure on the top tier of the stadium waving his arms and descending at speed to the track below shouting, "We've won," and City were promoted. To bring me down to earth the Russian coach came over and said, "I have a problem, six athletes, all are under 52.00 seconds and I do not know which four to pick." Some problem, as only a handful of British girls have ever reached such a standard.

The presentation celebrations were amazing; over five hundred guests were invited to an outdoor banquet and disco on converted tennis courts on a warm Greek evening. As the night drew on, the athletes became more boisterous, and the Russian girls treated everyone to a Cossack dance on top of one of the tables. One of our team took up the challenge, and after winning the duel, with a victory gesture fell through the table. When the early hours arrived the scene was carnage with the destruction of about sixty chairs and tables, but there was no hooliganism as such, everything having been regarded in fun.

The year finished on a sad note when in November 1999, Harold Wilson, our Secretary for forty-one years, passed away. Harold and his brother Walter were the founding fathers of Sale Harriers, seeing the club rise from a humble cotton dump track at Crossford Bridge to the top of British athletics. He was no mean athlete in his younger days, and incredibly, won a number of national veteran titles at the age of seventy-three. Harold, a member for over seventy years, was the perfect gentleman, kindly, courteous, always with a smile on his face and will never be forgotten in the club's history.

Finishing runners-up in the domestic Senior Jubilee Cup, we missed out in 2000, but again represented Great Britain in 2001 when the competition was held in Madrid in intense heat. Once more it was a question of taking on national sides, and we were relegated to the Second Division.

We were invited to Rennes in 2001 as UK Under 20s champions, and my mind went back eleven years to when we tied with Hungary and won the Cup for the first time on count back. On this occasion we scored the same number of points as Slovenia and both were awarded the same number of gold medals, but our opponents collected more silver and won the trophy. However, we were instrumental in promoting Great Britain back to the First Division, and Jean Kehoe, our Team Manager, received her baptism of overseas competition.

Our reward was an unforgettable visit to Moscow in 2002 in the company of all the top Eastern Bloc countries, and we did exceptionally well to come fourth.

After a nightmare of securing visas, we arrived in Moscow for what promised to be a very memorable trip. The team were accommodated in a hotel 14 storeys high, half on one side and half on the other, with no connecting doors. So, if I wished to communicate with Jean, a coach or athlete I had to travel down 14 flights in the lift, cross the hallway and travel up 14 flights to the other side. There were no sheets on the beds, the bathroom and WC were foul smelling, and the water was brown. Breakfast the following morning consisted of cold rice with tomato sauce and weak, lukewarm coffee. The only way to keep spirits high was to joke about the situation, buy food elsewhere, and make the best of the accommodation. The response was magnificent, and superb team spirit carried us through a well organised athletic meeting the following day, with a creditable result.

To make some amends, a farewell banquet was held in a restaurant situated on the Kremlin Walls, but to get there we had to walk quite a distance on a freezing night with the girls scantily dressed for the occasion. The evening was a great success, and the food and entertainment excellent. Due to the time difference, we had most of the Sunday to ourselves.

Thanks to American dollars, we persuaded our driver to borrow his coach for a tour of the famous sights and engaged a well-known guide to accompany us on a not-to-be-forgotten tour that included a trip to Red Square and the Kremlin. We were lucky that Lenin's tomb was open without the usual impossible queues, and some of the girls, who were not exactly history students, expected to see the body of John Lennon (not Lenin) complete with steel glasses. Afterwards I kept my promise to treat the girls to McDonald's to compensate somewhat for the poor food we endured over the weekend. The coach then took us on to the airport, and we arrived home safely, but exhausted.

We returned to learn that we would be given a civic reception by the Lord Mayor of Manchester in acknowledgement of winning all the top domestic athletic honours within a year. These comprised the UK League, the National Senior Cup, the National Under 20s Cup, the National Senior Cross Country, and the National Senior Road Relay titles. The trophies were put on display at the town hall, and we were received by the Mayor Elect, Roy Walters. It was fitting that he would be in the number one job at the Commonwealth Games the following year.

As a club, we played a prominent role before and during the Games, including management, coaching, officiating, media work, and training supervision for the various participating countries. Additionally, we provided well over one hundred volunteers and organised a special track and field meeting as a rehearsal to try out the athletic facilities. No fewer than twelve of our athletes had qualified to compete in the Games, and Lorraine Shaw had the honour of winning the first gold medal for England in the hammer. Contrary to her usual calm self, she went berserk, celebrating in style once she realised she had won. Darren Campbell and Allyn Condon also picked up gold medals in the 4 x 100 metres relay team, and all our athletes performed with distinction. In the build-up to the Games, a number of our athletes and myself were featured on camera in the official opening of the track. We enacted a training session as part of the ceremony and later lined up to meet Tony Blair. It must have been big thrill for youngsters with modest backgrounds to shake hands with the prime minister.

In 2002 we won the senior trophy in Amsterdam, securing promotion back to the First Division, and this particular year highlighted another page in athletic history. We became the first club to contend three European Championships in the same year, the Senior Track and Field, the Under 20s Track and Field, and the Senior Cross Country.

The seniors travelled to Valencia in 2003 where the competition was even more fierce and came in seventh, relegating us to the Second Division again. No British team could hope to do very much better with the existing rules, but the experience of competing against world class athletes was invaluable.

Jean took charge of the Under 20s team in 2003 held in Koper, Slovenia, ably assisted by the event coaches as my wife and I were celebrating our golden wedding anniversary in Venice, not too far away. We came in sixth with a much changed team, and in 2004 held the same position in Gateshead to maintain premier status. This was the second time the UK had hosted the European Cup since we held the meeting in 1990. From the inaugural match in Belgium in 1986 the competition had now escalated to sixty nations participating in four venues all over Europe.

It was the turn of the seniors to visit Slovenia in 2004, this time to Maribor, with no fewer than seven of our top internationals missing, leaving us with a threadbare squad. More disaster followed when Danielle Halsall passed out on the outward journey and had to receive medical treatment en route at Frankfurt. The pilot contacted the medical centre on the ground, and when we landed, a doctor and paramedic crew were waiting for us. After assuring them that I would meet any relevant costs, Danielle was lifted on to a stretcher and transported by ambulance to the centre in the company of Shelley Holroyd and myself. As I did not know what lay ahead, I told the team to check in at the departure gate for Graz in Austria, the nearest airport to Maribor, and wait. Another residential doctor was waiting for us, and after diagnosing a nose and ear infection, Danielle received an injection that helped her recover, and she was placed on a saline drip to stabilise her condition.

It was now a question of whether we would make the connecting flight, and the authorities were made aware of the situation in order to provide emergency measures. With little time left, the doctor issued a flying certificate, but not without me paying for all the medical charges incurred. Climbing adjacent stairs to the main airport, an electric buggy was waiting for us with a security guard driver. Shelley clutched Danielle at the rear of the vehicle and I rode with the driver stage coach fashion, racing across the airport and scattering people, shouting, "Out of the way," warnings to the departure gate, just in time to board the aircraft with the rest of the team.

On the day of the athletic event, the sprint relay was held unusually early, and we were chasing a club record when, with 40 metres to go, our final leg runner fell to the ground with a torn hamstring. This left only twelve athletes to contest eighteen events but, against the odds, with a magnificent display of guts and wonderful team spirit, we finished a great fourth, avoiding relegation for our country to a lower division.

In the same year, Darren Campbell became Sale's first Olympic gold medallist with the victorious British 4 x 100 metres relay team in Athens, where Lorraine Shaw (hammer) and Philippa Roles (discus) also took part.

10

As a legacy to the most successful Commonwealth Games of all time, the City Council envisaged a super athletic club to reflect the image of Manchester. Also aided by the inspiration of the Games, it was an ideal opportunity to promote a healthier lifestyle for its people through sport. Alan Robertshaw arranged a meeting high up in the Velodrome with Jimmy Quigley, one of the council's driving forces, and myself to consider the possibility of the council and club joining forces in a partnership deal to achieve these objectives.

We agreed to the idea in principle, and after a series of debates between both parties, we decided that we could work together in harmony. The newly constructed stadium and indoor arena provided a perfect base to enhance the club's standards and help our coaches organise development in the local community.

One problem was that a super club had to be established to identify with the city, and although Manchester had been added to the name Sale Harriers some years ago, this was insufficient. We felt we could not let a name, world famous for nearly a century, be sacrificed, and yet we could see the council's point of view. After months of investigation and negotiation, in 2005 we finally broke through the legal barrier and registered City of Manchester Athletics for our senior track & field teams, retaining Sale Harriers Manchester for all other divisions of the club. From 2006 onwards, the name of Manchester rang out in all major stadiums, home and abroad, accompanied by unrivalled success. The super club had arrived.

Such glory was tinged with sadness when, in February 2004, my old friend and confederate, Bill Nicholls, passed away, followed by Jack Tyrell in April 2005. I still think of them both with great fondness and gratitude for the friendship and invaluable support they gave me throughout the years. Frank Starkie, our club secretary, probably the best administrator in athletics, suddenly died in March 2006, and Alan Robertshaw, the man who brought me into the club way back in 1969, passed away in June 2006 after a long illness so bravely fought. To lose four such wonderful, knowledgeable friends in such a short space of time was heartbreaking and my sporting life became a lonely place.

In 2006, I was elected club president, continuing my dual role in team management and executive duties, but with more leadership responsibilities. Membership now numbered 900 plus, and we operated over three tracks.

Since 2004 the women's team had won the UK League First Division three more times, making it twenty-one championships in the past thirty-four years, being runners-up on eight other occasions. The only blemish was in 2006 when we conceded the title to Edinburgh, who were the first club to win the League way back in 1975. It may seem like sour grapes, but we only lost by one point relating to the first match, which coincided with the England vs Jamaica football match at Old Trafford. A number of athletes, ours included, were held up by massive queues on the M6 motorway and missed their events, whereas the Edinburgh team had stayed overnight locally and had no traffic problems.

I had been fortunate to have participated in every UK League meeting since its inception, and if I made the first fixture in the 2008 season it would be one hundred successive appearances in thirty-three years without missing a match. Finishing in 2007 with ninety-nine appearances, I had to wait agonizingly until May 2008 to score my century at the opening meeting in Birmingham. When the big day arrived, my phone rang at 7.30 a.m. with the caller informing me that there had been a fatal accident on the M6. The motorway had been closed, blocking the road to Birmingham. I contacted as many athletes as possible and set out only to encounter one hazard after the other.

I began to believe I would never make it. However, some hours later, with a sigh of relief, I finally arrived at the stadium whereupon it was somewhat embarrassing to hear my century being announced over the loud speaker.

After winning the Northern Regional Services to Athletics award, I was honoured to be nominated for the national finals and attended the inaugural English Athletics National Awards at Solihull with Doris in October 2008. This was to be a special occasion, because the first Hall of Fame inductions were also being held to acknowledge legends of athletics. In a glittering evening, Fuz Ahmed, the husband of Sale high jumper Julie Crane, together with our own Darren Campbell, did a great job as masters of ceremony, and Sebastian Coe, Daley Thompson, Roger Bannister, Steve Ovett, and Sally Gunnell were all inducted. It was a memorable affair, and I enjoyed renewing acquaintances with Ann Packer, her husband Robbie Brightwell, and David Hemery, among others.

The last award of the evening went to my old friend and mentor Wilf Paish for his services to athletics. In a long distinguished career, he was national coach for many years, an outstanding author, and world famous for his achievements, which included taking Tessa Sanderson to an Olympic gold medal and Peter Elliott to a silver. His huge technical and physiological knowledge is unequalled, and Wilf received a standing ovation when he rose to collect the award. It was a privilege to make the last three and finish runner-up to such a remarkable man whose friendship I will always cherish.

The year ended in majestic fashion with the club being honoured by a civic reception. Instead of this being held at the Manchester Town Hall we invited the Lord Mayor to the City of Manchester stadium to our celebration evening held annually to thank the army of volunteers who support the club throughout the year. Mavis Smitheman, the Lord Mayor, with her multicoloured hair and love of sport, paid tribute to the men's and women's teams, presented awards for the 2008 Young Athletes of the Year, and recognised the five youngsters who had done so well in the Commonwealth Youth Games in India.

So culminated thirty-nine years in athletics from the very early days as an interested parent to nearly four decades of ups and downs, trials and tribulations, fun, agony, and triumphs. I have colourful memories of a sport that is tough and uncompromising and feel in some way that I have contributed to the welfare of athletics. I would also like to think I have made a difference to the lives of many.

My grateful thanks go to my secretary, Janice Walton,
who took down every word in shorthand and immaculately
transcribed the manuscript of the book.

Lightning Source UK Ltd.
Milton Keynes UK
30 June 2010

156319UK00001B/67/P